The Greatest Escapes of World War II

THE GREATEST ESCAPES
OF WORLD WAR II

ROBERT BARR SMITH
AND LAURENCE J. YADON

Guilford, Connecticut

An imprint of Rowman & Littlefield

Distributed by NATIONAL BOOK NETWORK

British Library Cataloguing in Publication Information Available

Library of Congress Cataloging-in-Publication Data Available

ISBN 978-1-4930-2502-2 (paperback)
ISBN 978-1-4930-2663-0 (e-book)

♾™ The paper used in this publication meets the minimum requirements of American National Standard for Information Sciences—Permanence of Paper for Printed Library Materials, ANSI/NISO Z39.48-1992.

CONTENTS

FOREWORD

IT'S NO SHAME TO BE TAKEN PRISONER IN TIME OF WAR, although soldiers often think it is. War has always been the province of uncertainty and confusion. When something goes wrong in a major way, as Americans used to say, "There's hell to pay and no pitch hot." The price of uncertainty and confusion is often enemy success and your own captivity.

A lot of very good soldiers in the American Revolution looked around and asked their comrades, "Why, the Massachusetts boys were supposed to be up on that ridge behind us; who are those fellers in the red coats?"

Although the pace of war is much faster than it used to be, a few things remain the same. The first rule of being captured is to escape if you can. That duty is recognized by the Geneva Conventions. In World War II, captured Allied soldiers found vast differences in treatment depending on whose flag flew over prison headquarters: If your camp was run by one of the German armed forces—as it generally was—your treatment would be relatively humane. But if the camp command was Gestapo, you were in for a very bad time. And if the Japanese flag flew over the *Komandantur*, you were almost surely in a suburb of Hell.

Conditions in the Japanese camps were brutal and primitive. Many men died in them, from deliberate brutality, illness, or a combination of those two killers. Many other prisoners died on the freighters—the "hellships"—that took prisoners to Japan or other places close to the center of the empire. They were not marked as carrying prisoners as they should have been, so many of the prisoners died miserably when the ships were unwittingly sunk by Allied submarines or aircraft.

Escape was a constant subject of conversation, no matter where a man was confined, and planning went on incessantly in most camps. There was no lack of courage and determination, but there were some very formidable obstacles.

The greatest of these barriers were in Asia. First off, there was the simple fact that most Allied prisoners were Caucasian, who had no chance of blending into the local population. Likewise, there was the matter of language: In Europe, many of the POWs spoke some German or French, or could masquerade as a citizen of an area of which little was generally known by the occupiers. They could, for instance, pretend to be a Bulgarian or Serbian. There was no such chance in Asia.

In both Europe and Asia, there was also the simple obstacle of distance. Asian escapes were particularly frustrating; if you managed to break out of a camp in Formosa, for example, where was there to go? Escapers and evaders—those never caught—had an immense distance to travel through a maze of restrictions, replete with endless checking and questioning and a plethora of forms and passes and permits. Prison camp forgers had to become masters of such things, including their frequent changes.

Then there was the matter of clothing. Uniforms wouldn't work, of course, and that was all most men had. And so amateur prison tailors became quite expert at transmogrifying uniforms into grubby civilian attire or even business suits, and sprucing up found or purloined civilian clothing. Civilian buttons were collected and hoarded, and civilian shoes were a jewel beyond price.

In addition to your identification documents, labor permit, travel papers, and the like, much of it requiring photos, you also needed maps and border-crossing information to chart your course to safety, and the information needed to be as detailed as possible. For example, about half the small towns in Germany have a name ending in *stadt*, *dorf*, *feld*, or *heim*, and in many cases there are several towns of the same name. As an escaper, it was critical to know which *Schweinsdorf*—pig village—you had to get to: There was one in Silesia, another in Saxony, and one in Franconia at least, maybe more. If your timetable puts you in Obersdorf at 0900, is it the village down the road or the identically named town 150 kilometers away?

It was critical to have—or at least have access to—such mundane items as railroad timetables. If you were going to run into curfews or other travel restrictions you needed to know what, where, and when they were. You needed money.

Once the break was made, assuming it was successful, it was only a matter of time until the escape was discovered. That was generally a short time, since at least one formation was held daily—in German camps, it was *appell*—muster—at which everybody was supposed to be accounted for. There were some ingenious ways of delaying that, such as the British custom of using "ghost" prisoners to stand in formation for the escapers, but discovery in time was inevitable. Since the European camps were generally deep in Germany, even getting to France or Belgium, where there were active undergrounds to help, was a chancy, time-consuming effort.

Both Britain and America helped with organizations specifically designed to assist escapers: For Britain it was MI9; for the United States, MIS-X. Once Allied prisoners got to friendly ground, like France, there were also thousands of ordinary citizens willing to lay their lives on the line to help, if only with a hot meal, some fresh clothing, a safe place to get some badly needed sleep, or precious information about the doings of the detested *Boche* (Germans).

Our book does not purport to deal with all the escapes of WWII. There were thousands of attempts; more than a few were successful. We have dealt exclusively with escapes by Allied prisoners. There were some by Axis prisoners, virtually all with a signal lack of success. A brief mention of a few of them, however, is difficult to omit.

Take, for example, the break from the American camp at Papago, a part of Phoenix, Arizona. By early 1944, the camp was inhabited by some three thousand Germans, mostly *Kriegsmarine* (German sailors), including a contingent of U-boat officers. *Unterseeboat* officers tended to be hard-nosed folks, and that was particularly true of the most senior of them, Captain Juergen Wattenberg, nicknamed "super Nazi." He was a two-time loser, having been part of the *Graf Spee* disaster at the River Plate, and the sinking of his own *U-162*, sent to the bottom by the Royal Navy in the Caribbean in late 1942.

The camp command made it easy for Wattenberg, who chose a blind spot inside the camp to start his tunnel. The dirt was spread out inside attics, flushed down toilets, added to small gardens, and spread over the volleyball field. Nobody noticed, although the alert camp provost marshal vainly called attention to the blind spot.

At last, two days before Christmas in 1944, covered by much raucous noise and loud singing, Wattenberg and twenty-four others got clean away. That was Saturday, and because there was no roll call on Sunday, the Germans had a long lead. Or should have had, but while some headed for Mexico, some hid out in a nearby cave. Others surrendered within a few days, having quickly had a bellyful of hunger, cold, and rain.

One got himself arrested when he stopped to wash his underwear in a canal—a task passing cowboys thought odd—and Wattenberg was pinched after he had a meal in a Phoenix hotel and then asked directions of a street cleaner. His German accent gave him away, and he was back in Papago with all the rest of the escapers.

The Germans were equally disappointed by an attempt to spring four U-boat officers from a camp in Canada, including Otto Kretschmer of *U-99*, one of the real submarine "aces" of the war. The German Admiralty arranged this one, delivering messages via the Red Cross. The Canadians were watching, however, and monitored the whole operation, which required laborious tunneling and dirt-hiding, in the course of which the diggers managed to overload and collapse a barracks ceiling.

And then, just as the date for the great escape arrived, the guards and Royal Canadian Mounted Police moved in, arrested everybody, and blocked the tunnel. The only man to elude them escaped over the wall using, of all things, a homemade zipline. He managed to get to the point at which the escapers were supposed to be picked up by *U-536*. Her captain had smelled a rat, however, skipped the rendezvous, and eluded the Canadian depth charges.

None of the prisoners got away, and *U-536* was sunk by British and Canadian warships the following month.

The Germans did better in September of 1943, on the Gran Sasso down in the Appenines. Feckless Italian dictator Benito Mussolini had been deposed in late July and was being held by the new Italian government in the Hotel Campo Imperatore, guarded by 200 men. Hitler was determined to rescue his erstwhile comrade-in-fascism and sent in his first team, German

Fallschirmjaeger—paratroopers—and some *Schutzstaffel* (SS) personnel led by tough, able, SS officer Otto Skorzeny.

Because the hotel was reachable only by cable car, the raiders landed by glider with only minor injuries. The guard force was ordered by an Italian general to stand down, and *il Duce* was rescued without a shot being fired. There followed this memorable conversation:

Skorzeny: *"Duce*, the *Fuehrer* has sent me to set you free!"
Mussolini: "I knew that my friend would not forsake me!"

Or something like that. Or maybe nobody said anything at all, and the heroic speeches by both men were invented, for the Third Reich needed all the good propaganda it could get just then.

Skorzeny flew Mussolini off the mountain in a Fiesler Storch liaison plane, *il Duce* eventually flew into Berlin to Hitler's welcome, Skorzeny and the SS got the lion's share of the credit (although the *Fallschirmjaeger* had done most of the work), and the "friends" had another year or so of life.

The German navy—or rather the interned crew of a civilian liner—tried another escape at Fort Stanton, New Mexico, in November 1942. This time, the internment camp was run for civilians and staffed by the U.S. Border Patrol. There were several escape attempts; all failed because of the remoteness of the camp.

Only once was there any excitement: A fleeing group of four Germans was spotted by a rancher while they were "taking a bath in a mountain stream," and followed up by a local posse. One of the POWs had come by a pistol; accordingly, some shooting ensued. The Germans lost and went back to jail, one with a brand-new hole in him.

The Allied escapers, on the other hand, were aided by a wide circle of selfless helpers, men who had little or no prospect of getting a chance at escape themselves but took long chances to help their fellow prisoners through the wire.

Generally each camp or large subcamp had an Escape Committee—often called the X Committee—which coordinated effort and allocated material assets. Everybody helped out: the men who dug tunnels, the "Penguins" who got rid of the dirt, the spies, the watchers, the tailors, the forgers, and the thieves who stole whatever anybody else needed.

A small percentage of the men who tried to escape ultimately reached friendly lines. But as one British escaper commented, their efforts, even if they failed, at least cost Germany many millions of marks in expenses to shore up their prison camps, plus thousands of men to guard prisoners and pursue escapers, men who might otherwise have been fighting the Allies.

The urge to be free and get back in the war was the primary motivation for these men who took long chances and risked their lives to escape—but there was also the very real desire to jerk the German or Japanese chain: "Take that, you bastards, we're still in this war."

They surely were.

Chapter One

Tom, Dick, and Harry

Stalag Luft III was considered to be an especially important link in the vast chain of German prisoner-of-war camps, if only because of the great number of very important prisoners it held. As the Allied air offensive against *Festung Europa* gained in strength and intensity, an increasing number of Royal Air Force (RAF) and U.S. Army/Air Force (USAAF) aircrew were forced to bail out or crash-land in German-held territory.

Highly trained aircrew were a precious commodity to the Allies. They took a long time to train—especially the pilots—and, accordingly, the British government put a high price on training them to avoid capture altogether or getting them out of enemy confinement and returned to duty. As early as December of 1939, Great Britain created MI9, an organization dedicated in large part to aiding the escape of airmen from the Germans.

In partnership with America's MIS-X, a clandestine organ with similar objectives, MI9's operatives worked as far away from home as China, parachuted into hostile places all over the world, and helped get out as many people as they could. All kinds of people owed their freedom to the men and women of MI9, but aircrew remained very high priority.

By and large, these airmen were a smart and enterprising lot and the most unwilling guests of the Germans; they promptly became a gross pain in the neck for their captors, commonly called "goons" by the prisoner population. A great many of the aircrew ended up at the camp called Stalag Luft III. It was a sprawling installation, close to the Polish border, some hundred miles south of Berlin and near the provincial town of Sagan.

The first couple of hundred POWs, British and American, arrived in the spring of 1942 and were confined in a section of Stalag Luft III called the North Compound. The compound was an area almost exactly a quarter-mile square, surrounded by the customary guard towers and two barbed-wire fences. The inside fence carried an electric charge, enough to alert the guards that somebody was fiddling with the fence. The second band of fence was more formidable still, no less than nine feet tall and strung with twenty strands of wire.

As if that were not security enough, there were also coils of barbed wire in the twenty feet or so between the fences, night guards who patrolled the fences, and more guards with unfriendly dogs inside the compound itself. It might have looked escape-proof to some peaceful civilians but not to the new residents.

Escape planning began almost immediately upon the prisoners' arrival, led by Squadron Leader Roger Bushell, RAF, head of the brand-new escape apparatus, the "X Committee." "Big X" as he was known, was older than most of his fellow prisoners but still a daring man and a born leader. One of the treasured parts of the prewar decor of his former squadron's mess was a road sign he had amputated while landing his aircraft for a drink at a rural pub.

He was surrounded by kindred spirits, mostly young men willing to try anything to escape and get back in the war, or just, as the British put it, to "cock a snook" at the Germans. One of these young firebrands was American-born Major Johnny Dodge, a globe-trotting adventurer who had joined the British forces—first navy, then army—and become a British subject in 1915.

He was twice wounded in World War I and won a chestful of decorations, starting with the Distinguished Service Cross. Spending the years between wars adventuring around the world, he ended up in the British Expeditionary Forces (BEF) in France in 1940 and was captured. He was first sent to another camp, where he was magically turned into an RAF officer by a stroke of the commandant's pen and moved to Stalag Luft III.

He was Bushell's kind of man.

So was Jimmy James, an RAF navigator who had walked some fifteen miles with a broken ankle through occupied Holland before Dutch collaborators sold him out to the Germans. There were dozens more, all eager to escape, ready for any scheme that offered even a glimmer of a chance of success. Most of them were already veterans of at least one attempt to escape by the time they reached Stalag Luft III.

Bushell's madcap side didn't detract from his cool judgment; he would serve his fellow prisoners well. Bushell and the X Committee made a couple of intelligent decisions at the outset: First, use of the magic word "tunnel" was *verboten* for everybody; it was too easy to slip and say it where one of the Germans might hear.

Second, trying to go out over the wire and through the guards and the dogs was obviously a very bad idea; it was plainly not going to work. What chance there was would be to go under the fences, to dig and dig deeply, and that was best done at several points, without putting all their eggs in one basket. Accordingly, the committee decreed that there would be not one but three tunnels, and they would be called simply "Tom," "Dick," and "Harry." (In time, "George" was begun, but that's another tale.)

All prisoners would instantly recognize what was meant by the simple name; no German would have a clue. Take "Harry," for example: It was somebody's first name, that was all. And if one tunnel were found by the guard force, or even two of the three, with any luck at all there would still remain a chance for escape.

There were obvious problems. The barracks floors were deliberately built some two feet above the surface of the ground, to give the goons plenty of room to check for tunnel entrances. But you couldn't very well build latrines and showers two feet off the ground, and the Germans had also realized that there had to be some sort of hard foundation for the barracks stoves.

So, the brickwork foundations were the starting place. The diggers would use chunks of iron from old stoves, sections of tin can as shovels, and chisels improvised from table knives. And their hands.

For Dick, the starting place was a washroom drain. It was about eighteen inches square and set right in the middle of the floor. The tunnel, however, was started well inside the drain, a block of its concrete carefully chipped out of its side, big enough for a man to crawl through the wall of the drain into the soft earth around it and be about his digging.

A new concrete block to fill the hole was carefully cast from mix German workmen had left behind and had been liberated by prisoners along with all manner of other useful things sent by the X Committee. With the new block in place—the cracks painstakingly filled in with a mixture of soap and dust—and the grill on the washroom floor replaced, Dick was invisible. Similar magic produced Harry, hidden beneath a stove in another barracks block. Tom was started in what was called "a dark corner" of a washroom in still another block.

Which brought the Escape Committee to an even more difficult problem: what to do with the "spoil," the copious amounts of dirt the three tunnels would produce. You couldn't just dump it anyplace, for once the diggers got only slightly below the surface of the soil, the color of the spoil changed dramatically: No longer a nice quiet, unobtrusive dirt-colored dirt, it came up a bright yellow sand. You couldn't just pile the stuff up and hope nobody noticed; it stuck out like a sore thumb in any quantity.

A British pilot named Peter Fanshawe suggested the answer. We must scatter it, he said, scatter it in very small quantities, amounts so tiny they won't be noticed. It would take great care and much organization. It also took equipment, long pockets improvised from pajama bottoms, long underwear, and other trousers. These you carefully filled with spoil, which you then very carefully dribbled away in very small quantities, hanging the bag down your pant leg and walking about trying to look innocent while you pulled gently on a drawstring and bled the bag very slowly of its contents.

Some of the tell-tale yellow sand could be hidden in the little gardens the prisoners were allowed to cultivate. The "dirt-colored" dirt dug out of the gardens could be mixed in with the yellow stuff to dilute it and make it easier to spread. The earth-hiding operation took lots of earth-spreaders, but there was no shortage of men eager to help. They were called "Penguins."

To keep the amount of spoil to a minimum and speed up progress, the tunnels had to be as small as possible, so narrow that only a single man could work at the face at once. Behind him was another man to whom he shoved his gleanings. The second man loaded the dirt into a little wagon with ropes attached to both ends; a tug on the rope signaled another prisoner, who hauled the cart back to the tunnel entry. As the tunnels got longer, there would be even more men engaged in moving dirt back to the tunnel entry.

And the longer the tunnels grew, the harder the work got. The tunnels were always hot, the air foul, in spite of improvised ventilation in the form of a sort of homemade bellows also produced by the prisoners. And the tunnels were dark, dark as the pits of hell, even with a primitive lighting system, a sort of candle-lamp fueled by fat skimmed from mess-hall soup and from margarine and food fat purloined from the kitchens. A piece of cord made a simple wick. In time, the tunnels would be lit with power bootlegged from the prison system, but until then the dim, stinking, primitive lamplight would have to do.

What to do about possible interference by the guards? Ordinary caution helped, of course, eternal caution in every word and even the simplest action. So did the alarm system inside the tunnels, tin cans filled with a handful of pebbles, actuated by a long string running along the ceiling of the tunnels. At the approach of a guard uncomfortably close to the tunnel entry, a little tug on the string brought strict silence. Other prisoners formed a surveillance system, keeping track of where the goons were and where they were probably going.

The diggers had to be endlessly vigilant about their everyday prison clothing as well. No trace of the tell-tale yellow sand could be allowed outside where guard personnel might see it, either piled on the ground or smeared on a digger's clothing. Accordingly, everybody in the tunnels worked either naked or in long johns.

Tunnel Tom was a good illustration of the system in action. The spoil came back down the tunnel and up to the washroom in cans. These were dumped on the floor on a blanket tended by American Tom Minskewitz, who filled the trouser-leg bags of the Penguins. They then went about their casual strolling, their gardening, or their group masquerades. The blanket kept the washroom floor clear of the deadly yellow sand while the distributors' bags were filled.

The dirt distribution systems were many and varied. American Jerry Sage, for example, had organized a sort of drill team—forty men or so—as a means of exercise and passing the time. These men practiced their drills assiduously with ten or twelve earth-scatterers marching in the middle of their formation. Some of the spectators at prisoner volleyball games also left a little yellow sand behind them. The system worked.

For a while, at least. And then a prisoner got careless, a Penguin who unloaded too much of his bag of yellow sand in one place while standing alone a little distance away from the crowd at a volleyball match. Before anybody could pick it up or scatter it, it was spotted by a guard. The goons now knew that there was digging underway someplace.

An orgy of searching found nothing, however; the Germans even drove trucks up and down in the compound, obviously intending to cave in any tunnels; they could not know that Tom, Dick, and Harry were thirty feet below them. The goons even went so far as to hide a couple of their men in the ceiling of one prison block, presumably to eavesdrop on prisoners' guilty language. There were almost daily barracks searches.

Then came the Germans' maximum effort: an incursion by about a hundred soldiers, who industriously dug a four-foot-deep ditch across the compound and then began poking steel rods down its bottom, obviously probing for the roof of any tunnel. There was some excitement among the searchers when one probe hit something hard. Their prize turned out to be a rock, to the intense amusement of their prisoner audience.

The guards got nothing except acute embarrassment, but the need for increased caution was obvious to the diggers, and the work slowed dramatically. One solution was to stop work on Tunnel Dick and turn it into a dump for the treacherous sand.

Abandoning Dick had another advantage: now, a few pieces at a time, the diggers could also remove and reuse Dick's timbering, the mattress slats from the beds of a good many prisoners.

The slats, some four thousand of them, were only part of the colossal infusion of German property converted by the prisoners to serve the Allied war effort. Included were hundreds of pieces of eating utensils, over a thousand feet of rope, hundreds of blankets and towels, and some 1,400 tin cans.

Probably the most important loot were two large rolls of electrical wire. These had been left on the ground by a German electrician while he perched on a ladder wiring something else and were casually picked up and boldly liberated by a passing member of the escape team. The two rolls became the heart of the tunnel lighting system; no longer were the diggers required to grope about in primordial gloom and the stench of smoldering grease.

The run of good luck was interrupted by a sad event: the transfer of the American prisoners to another camp not long before the projected time of the tunnels' completion. The Yanks, as the British called them, had contributed much to what would later become known as the Great Escape; now they could not share in it. If their transfer was a profound disappointment at the time, time would reveal it as a mixed blessing.

The work went on until Tom was making as much as ten feet a day; it was almost into the woods surrounding the compound, and then the blow fell; the Germans sent a work party out to cut down trees and brush until the shelter of the woods had been pushed back a hundred feet or so. Worse was to come.

A surprise search discovered the entrance to Tom. While a guard was painstakingly tapping one of the washroom floors, his little metal rod lodged in a minute crack. He pushed on with his careful inquiry, more guards pitched in, and the result was the discovery and destruction of Tom. A guard who crawled to the end and back is said have taken a half-hour for the round trip.

It was a blow, after all the sweat and the filth, the danger and the sacrifice, but Bushell cast it in the right light. "We're going ahead," he said, and added, "we still have two tunnels; the Germans probably think we don't have any." And so, although the Escape Committee suspended digging operations for a while, mostly because of bitter cold weather, they started again in earnest when the new year arrived.

Harry now advanced as many as ten or twelve feet a day, until it reached almost 350 feet. Since the distance to the forest was estimated at 335 feet, it was at last time to dig another direction . . . up. This time there would be no last-minute disappointment, for the initial upward dig hit what the prisoners had long hoped for: tree roots. And at last, in March, a metal rod pushed into the roof of the upward leg of the tunnel broke through with only six inches to go to the surface.

Freedom was just half a foot away.

Last-minute planning also called for two things: the best weather possible at this time of year and, if possible, a moonless night. The Escape Committee settled on March 24.

While the digging had been going on, the forgers had been busy with all kinds of false documents, identity cards, and passes and paybooks and such, of which there seemed to be an endless variety. Nobody traveled in Nazi Europe without at least one such *ausweis*, generally more. Nobody could. Whatever disguise each escaper chose, his paper had to match; it had to have a convincing picture and the appropriate date stamp, and it had to appear wrinkled and a little faded with use.

Some of the forgers' raw materials came from goons hungry for decent cigarettes and other treasures from Red Cross parcels.

Trading was done on the barter system, of which the unit of measurement was the cigarette. Some required documents were improvised on the spot; for instance, quite useful official-looking stamps—without which no German document was complete—were created from boot soles. The necessary ID photographs were taken with a German officer's borrowed Leica, ostensibly for mailing home.

RAF flight lieutenant Tim Walenn had been a graphic artist as a civilian; he became forger-in-chief, responsible for producing the enormous quantity of paper: the men due to escape had chosen their identities and the costumes that matched them. They had necessarily also chosen their nationality. All the documents Walenn and his forgery crew produced had to match an escaper . . . and be both convincing and current.

Some prisoners spoke fluent French or German; some were native speakers of other tongues, like Polish and Dutch. Some British officers could manage no language save their own, at least not convincingly. These men chose identities that required a speech few Germans were likely to understand. Bulgarian was popular; one prisoner put it pretty well: "Nobody speaks Bulgarian except the Bulgarians, and they're 600 miles away"—which had a certain logic to it, although the Escape Committee turned that man down. At least two others did go out as Bulgarians, "forestry students"; that guise would at least give them a chance of accounting for themselves if the Germans caught them skulking about in the woods.

These men were part of the contingent called "hard-assers," men planning to make their escape cross-country, hiding where they could, living rough, traveling fast in what promised to be vile weather. At least the hard-assers didn't have to worry as much about inquisitive waiters and desk clerks, busybody train conductors, and nosy policemen.

The underground tailor shop also had much painstaking work to do before the break. Staffed mostly by Czech and Polish officers, the tailors turned out everything from business suits to German military uniforms to foreign workers' dungarees. Their work took immense care; you might get away with converting a military tunic to a civilian coat if you were very, very careful, but you had to pay the closest attention to every detail, even little things like buttons and stripes.

Compasses for the hard-assers were created by painstakingly magnetizing prisoners' razor blades, then breaking them into tiny slivers. Compass cases came from melted plastic phonograph records, and luminous compass points were created from the hands of the commandant's own alarm clock, purloined from his office. The genius who made these useful things was an Australian named Hake, whose finishing touch was stamping each of his compasses "Made in Stalag Luft III. Patent Pending." By the spring of 1944, he had turned out more than five hundred compasses.

Nobody would go out armed. Even had they been able to obtain weaponry, it would have done them little good in the middle of Fortress Europe. It would simply have gotten them killed, shot down during arrest, or murdered by the Gestapo later. Wits and careful preparation were the prisoners' weapons; they carried nothing more deadly than their prisoner dog tags, essential to any kind of decent treatment if they were recaptured.

Some elected to travel alone. Others went out in pairs or even slightly larger groups. There was some comfort in not being alone, and two or more prisoners could help each other. But large groups of prisoners were almost sure to attract more unwelcome attention than a man alone or a companionable pair.

Then came the hard part: How many prisoners could try the break, and how would they be selected? The committee made the tough calls, since the best estimates were that a total of no more than 200 to 220 POWs could make it through the tunnel in a single night, and more than 500 men wanted to go.

The first thirty were chosen as having the best chance for escape, because of some special quality, such as fluency in French or other languages. They would all travel by train, and the early start would help guarantee them time to get to the local railroad station in time to have their pick of trains.

Bushell and his committee would then hold a drawing for the remaining spaces, and these men would go out in the order in which their names had been drawn. The next twenty spaces were chosen from those who had worked hardest in the tunnel; ten more from the biggest contributors among the forgers and tailors and gadget-makers and Penguins. The rest of the 200 or so were chosen in a blind draw from everybody else who wanted to go. There was much disappointment.

At zero hour, the first seventeen men were poised at the head of the tunnel, waiting for it to be opened into the darkness and cool of the woods . . . and freedom. It was only then that they made the saddest discovery of all their days in the prison camps. The diggers' calculations had been in error . . . the shelter of the woods was still some ten feet away. And about forty short feet away to one side of the tunnel exit, in plain view, there was a sentry post, and it was manned.

Bushell had an enormous command decision to make, and just minutes to make it.

We go, he said; we can't wait another month. The risk in waiting for another favorable moon was too great. Every day of delay heightened the chance of a guard or an informant learning something, of a prisoner slipping. And now they had the exit hole to worry about.

And so the file of POWs traveled one by one down the long tunnel on the little trolley that had served to evacuate all that spoil, carefully holding their baggage out in front of them—the size and weight of what each man would carry had already been passed on by the Escape Committee.

At one point the electric lighting shut down for a half hour or so, courtesy of the Royal Air Force; some eight hundred British bombers were on their way to Berlin. The German capital was a hundred or so miles away, but the Germans regularly turned off the power of any city or town that might furnish a landmark to guide Allied aircraft to Berlin. If the shutdown pitched the tunnel into stygian gloom, it also extinguished the camp's exterior lighting, including the searchlights along the perimeter fence. That at least was some help to the escapers who had already reached the tunnel exit.

The exit itself was the first obstacle. The tunnel hatch was frozen shut in this miserably cold weather, and it took more than an hour in the gloom of the exit tunnel to break it loose.

Some of the baggage also caused problems, falling off or momentarily jamming the progress of the little trolley. It was much worse for RAF officer Tom Kirby-Green: his suitcase hung up on some of the tunnel's timbering and he was buried in a cave-in deep in the pitch-black tunnel. Frantic digging by the other prisoners got him out shaken and unhurt, but the process took the better part of an hour. More delay.

At the exit, each man climbed up through the exit hole, and crawled carefully past the sentry post. Once out and into the dubious safety of the woods, each man stood and cautiously walked away, and for a while the system worked perfectly.

The eightieth man in line (some sources differ as to this number) was a prisoner called Bob McBride. He was climbing up to the surface for his chance at liberty, when he heard a shot and the howl of a whistle, and when he hastily reached the surface, he found himself looking down the barrel of a Mauser rifle.

And so, after all the toil and worry, the sweat and the planning and the careful precautions, the rest of the escapers would not get to breathe free air after all. It was a bitter pill. Those who hadn't made it out hastily burned their false papers—"dozens of little bonfires" as one source put it—while others feasted hastily on their carefully hoarded bits of traveling food.

In the end, after a series of wild adventures, only three men finally reached safety, just three of the dozens who started out. Two were Norwegian officers, the third a Dutchman; all of them were intimately familiar with Europe, fluent in other languages. None of hard-assers made it; the bitter weather and deep snow made off-road travel impossible.

On the plus side, however, those who made it out and survived tasted a priceless bit of freedom and gave fits to the German jailers and hunters. One RAF man, Jimmy James, put it pretty well:

> *I climbed up the ladder and the first thing I saw were stars. I thought of the RAF motto—per Ardua ad Astra (through adversity to the stars). . . . I lost some good friends in that escape . . . some of the finest men I've ever known.*

Jimmie would survive the war, in spite of being part of no fewer than a dozen escape attempts.

Seventeen of the recaptured escapers were returned to Stalag Luft III. Four more were sent to the concentration camp at Sachsenhausen, near Frankfurt. All four dug their way out and won a few weeks more of freedom, only to be recaptured and returned to Sachsenhausen camp. Two more ended up in the maximum security of Colditz Castle.

Sadly, inexcusably, foully, some fifty were executed after capture, killings that were premeditated murder in the simplest sense. Hitler had initially decreed that all recaptured officers were to be executed, and only reduced the number slightly after pleas from several high-ranking officers—among them Goering and Field-Marshal Keitel—that such killings plainly violated the Geneva Conventions.

Since early 1944, the protection of the Geneva Conventions had been increasingly ignored by the German authority, in particular the Gestapo. Muller, the Gestapo chief, ordered (in secret, of course) that all recaptured escapers, except British and Americans, were to be taken to Mauthausen concentration camp and shot out of hand. This order was appropriately called Aktion Kugel, the "Bullet Decree."

Among the dead was Big X, Roger Bushell. Bushell was shot along with a fellow officer near Saarbrueken, Germany, by a pair of Gestapo men. Bushell and his companion had made some eight hundred miles in about ten hours by fast train. When their luck ran out, the two officers were only two hours from France, where they stood a good chance of getting help from the Resistance.

The man who killed Big X, Emil Schulz, survived the war. He did not, however, survive British justice. The second Gestapo murderer was killed before the fighting ended.

Jimmie James made it through the war, along with thousands of other inmates of Sachsenhausen. The commandant got a Himmler *Befehl* (directive, order) on the first of February 1945, directing the extermination of the entire prisoner population, but the British contingent survived courtesy of a friendly police inspector. The prisoners ended up in a comparative paradise, a town in the peaceful Dolomite Alps.

For most of the escapers, at least, the whole exercise had been well worth it, in spite of the hardship and danger and disappointment, in spite of the grief the murder of their comrades caused them. Spitfire pilot Sidney Dowse, already a veteran escaper before he left Harry behind him, put it this way: "We caused havoc to the Germans and tied up thousands if not millions of them in the search for us."

Another Spitfire pilot, New Zealander Mike Shand, said much the same thing:

> *It was worth it. I don't think any of us thought we'd make it back to England . . . but we had to do something. We did it to cause chaos behind enemy lines and that's exactly what we did.*

The end of captivity for Johnny Dodge was not only miraculous but bizarre. Pulled out of confinement by an SS officer, he was whisked off to Berlin, dressed in civilian clothes, housed in the ritzy Adlon Hotel, and wined and dined. The reason soon became clear. He was to carry a peace proposal to England and present it to his "kinsman," none other than Winston Churchill (they were not, in fact, related). The German offer itself served to demonstrate the surreal, phantom world that was Berlin at the end of the war: Hitler would settle for nothing less than a British guarantee that Germany's prewar boundaries would be maintained.

At the end of Dodge's long trip home, he did get to see Churchill, who entertained him at 10 Downing Street. Two days later, Germany surrendered unconditionally.

It seems appropriate to close with something St. Matthew wrote a very long time ago. It is a short writing only, and already appears in a couple of excellent books on the "great escape." That does not lessen its power a bit, and I shamelessly quote it again here, for what St. Matthew said fits precisely the spirit that moved and sustained the men of Stalag Luft III, the men who would not give up: "And fear not them that kill the body, and are not able to kill the soul." No matter how tough things got, no matter how dangerous, the souls of the men of Stalag Luft III never wavered.

Chapter Two

Before Their Very Eyes

EVEN IF YOU GOT AWAY FROM WHEREVER YOU WERE CONFINED, there was still a long way to go to find help from a local underground, a neutral border, or even a safe spot to sleep. But all of these troubles paled before the simple conundrum of just getting out of the camp where you were being held in the first place. Digging a tunnel was the first thought that occurred to most men; included in those men, however, were not only those who wanted to escape, but those men—German—who wanted to stop them.

The prison's defenses grew more and more complex, as the commandant and his subordinates tried to get ahead of the ever-resourceful prisoners, tried to plan against the prisoners' next ingenious tactics. One useful precaution was to build the POW barracks on stilts, rock, or concrete piers, leaving the area beneath the floor open to easy view, without obstacle. That way, any digger trying to tunnel would be as obvious as a spider on a mirror during the day or in the glaring searchlights of the watches of the night. Many camps also had seismographs buried around the perimeter at intervals, the better to alert the guard force to the vibrations of any attempt to dig an escape tunnel under the perimeter wire.

So it was at Stalag Luft III, a Luftwaffe camp for airmen of a dozen different nationalities, built at Sagan, south and west of Berlin. The rest of the camp's defenses were ordinary but challenging: guard towers and tall twin barbed-wire fences with a jungle of barbed wire tangled in the space between them.

There were formidable dogs who roamed the night, regular formations to account for the prisoners' whereabouts, seismographs to record any vibration from digging. Sometimes there were informants, and always there was the danger of sudden and repeated searches.

Nor could a camp ever be mistaken for a resort: At Stalag Luft III, there were exactly six faucets to provide water for close to a thousand men. There were bunks with thin hard pallets and food far below the standard for Allied forces out in the free world. One thing there was lots of: time, lots of time for plotting, lots of time for quiet work.

This story necessarily stars the men who successfully escaped. But it is also a tribute to the dozens of men who helped in various ways and to a few civilians on the outside. Everybody contributed; the credit belongs to them all.

The prisoners of Stalag Luft III were well organized for the business of escape. At the top was the Escape Committee, through whom all efforts had to be channeled and approved; a hair-brained scheme, discovered, could bring down others with a greater chance of success.

Other men were employed in scrounging supplies, maps, and documents. There were subcommittees of talented forgers, who produced quite convincing identification documents, passes, travel permits, ration cards, work permits, and the rest of the myriad documents essential to movement in wartime Germany and the occupied nations of Europe. Other men worked as lookouts, while others—the Penguins—disposed of tell-tale dirt dug to open tunnels toward the wire.

There was a volunteer to distract the ferocious dogs who roamed the compound at night while other men crawled out to steal building material. The volunteer was equipped with copious amounts of pepper in case he had to deal with a dog hand-to-hand, and other men were poised to distract the dogs by shouting lustily through holes in their huts' floors.

And there were a few useful "ghosts," prisoners not on anybody's roster. They would pretend to be anybody who needed to vanish temporarily; the ghosts stood in for men who had to be absent from *appell*—roll call—on the critical business of escape.

At Stalag Luft III, the problem of escape was about as complex as it got. There were two twelve-foot barbed wire fences separated about fifteen feet by a mass of loose, tangled barbed wire. There were the usual guard towers, and a number of seismographs dug in about fifteen feet below ground level. Inside the innermost fence was a wire about a foot off the ground; step over it, and you got shot. The guard towers were manned, and there were more sentries outside the wire.

All of that was bad enough, but what was worse was the structure of the barracks huts. Not only were they built clear of the ground on pilings, but the sandy soil on which they stood was by turns dry and crumbly, or wet and glutinous. The wet was tough to work and move in; the dry was light-colored and obvious when you tried to get rid of it. The surface sand and the sand beneath were of slightly different colors, which added to the difficulty of dumping what you dug.

The solution turned out to be both simple and complex. Why not simply start the tunnel out in the open, out in the yard in plain view of the guard towers? You couldn't just go out and start digging, of course; there had to be some sort of cover to protect the diggers going to and from their work, and some way to move and hide the earth they dug.

The answer required the willing help of a number of prisoners, and the expertise of a number of specialists. The spot chosen for the dig would be hidden by a vaulting horse, the sort of simple structure used in gymnastics. There would be prisoners in lines to vault over it and otherwise act athletic in the prison yard, and the diggers would ride out to work concealed within the horse, which would be equipped with removable poles for carrying purposes.

It would take at least four strong men to carry the horse out of the barracks and back in again. The horse was built by prisoner carpenters of materials as light as possible, but it still had to be strong enough to vault over and strong enough to support the weight of two or three men going in and out. And on the return trip it also had to support bags of "spoil," as the diggers called the removed dirt.

The bags were easy; they were fabricated from cut-off trouser legs, and the builders formed small hooks from scrap metal and fixed them to the horse's frame. A dozen bags could be carried at once. Another crucial piece of construction was the lid for the diggers' entry hole. It was a sort of tray, which was carefully fitted and filled with sandy soil identical to that around the hole; as a final touch it was sprinkled with a little more sand to blend in with the rest of the yard at the end of the working day.

The spoil was carefully distributed in the yard in tiny sprinkles by a number of prisoners, leaking it down their own pants legs onto the soil of the yard, enriching the prisoner-run garden, or even dumped down an *abort*, short for outhouse. And if any man of the team—especially the diggers—could not get back in time to stand an *appell*, a "ghost" took his place in the formation.

Timbering for the tunnel came from salvaged wood, pilfered here and there, like the supports from an old bathhouse, from which the well-organized operation of a rafter-pinching party got their loot with nary a dog's woof or a guard's shout.

Some timbering came from empty crates or even bed slats, a supply to which every prisoner was willing to contribute. Even so, timbering had to be carefully hoarded, for it was scarce and tough to purloin without being caught, even for the accomplished thieves of the escape teams.

The difference in soil coloration meant that the spoil had to be kept to a minimum. The tunnel had therefore to be as tiny as possible. And so one man dug alone, sweltering in hot air quickly going foul, driving a tiny tunnel in which he had to lie prone, usually working naked, unable to turn around. The spoil he sent back to the entry point of the excavation, using a crude conveyer made of a tin plate attached to cords by which the plate was pulled to the digging face and back. The second man bagged up the spoil, ready for removal at the end of the day.

Timbering—shoring up the tunnel—had to be done by one man lying on his back, carefully evening the sides of the tunnel, then inserting vertical supports and the overhead slats that made the roof. It was delicate work, and the man doing the work had to have steel nerves, knowing that even a small cave-in would pin him on his back, helpless and suffocating in pitch blackness.

The initial digging went well. The horse had passed muster when it was examined secretly one night by "ferrets" of the camp guard personnel. The prisoners had thoughtfully adorned the horse with strategically placed threads when it was carried indoors at night. The broken threads told them that the ferrets had inspected and found nothing suspicious.

There were other tunnel efforts going on at the same time elsewhere in the camp. One managed to cut through a six-inch concrete foundation slab, but came to grief when the guards suddenly descended on the work site with a hose; they blasted the area of the floor that concealed the trap door, and their assiduous washing exposed the outline of the trap. Those guards obviously knew a tunnel was being dug nearby; they were probably alerted by a reaction on the seismograph.

But the crew of diggers and vaulters and ghosts and spoil-dumpers carried on, and the goons—prisoner language referring to the guards—were not further alarmed. It is probable that the seismographs were not alerted, or the alerts were ignored because of a combination of very careful digging and by the continual ground-bashing of the vaulters. Other prisoners helped out by walking and running in the yard, throwing quoits, and otherwise acting athletic.

The vaulters dug out two shallow sand pits next to the horse, ostensibly to cushion the shock of a vaulter land with bare feet. No doubt the pits did so, but their real purpose was to mark the resting place of the horse, so that it was placed each day on exactly the same spot.

The tiny tunnel crept on toward the wire of the outside fence a little at a time, the digger of the team sweating in stygian gloom, breathing ever-fouler air, scraping away at the face of the tunnel with improvised tools. As the tunnel got longer and longer, the air supply got bad more quickly. That problem was partially solved by periodically building in what the diggers called a "bulge," a wide spot in which some air could accumulate before being crowded on forward to the sweating, gasping digger at the leading edge of the tunnel.

Meanwhile, the camp forgers were busy fabricating the essential documents. The escapers would be French engineering draftsmen, respectable but not highly technical positions. One British officer scheduled to escape could draw, and the second could speak quite fluent French, which gave them at least some authenticity. They could not be German, since the little German either of them spoke came out with a markedly un-German accent.

And so the forgers produced the essential paper that would make the escapers phony Frenchmen: identity documents, travel permits, work permits, whatever would normally be carried by foreigners of the middle class. The paper was high quality, and the seals appeared authentic, fine copies of the seals so beloved of the German bureaucracy.

One of the proofs of legitimate employment was copied from the real letterhead of a German metal hut builder. The sample had been stolen by a young Jewish girl and passed on to the camp's Escape Committee.

The escapers needed money, too—in this case, the real thing. The complexity of forging Reichsmarks was beyond the equipment of the forgery department; in any case, production of an obviously false bill was the quickest way to end up in the tender hands of the *Polizei*. Along with the money, the escapers would often get a small package of other essentials: soap and cigarettes (German, of course), a small compass and flashlight, and in case hasty document alterations were needed, a pen and ink.

Another set of artists turned their talents to the production of ersatz civilian clothing. The German camp command had no objection to prisoners receiving the uniforms of their own country; those, like the Red Cross packages, at least relieved a little of the strain on the already overburdened German economy that could ill afford to clothe its prisoners.

At least one prisoner received the dress uniform of a Royal Marine officer—although the prisoner had no connection with the Marines—and that fine garment was transmogrified into civvies. A British Airways trench coat became a civilian raincoat, a beret was fabricated from a blanket, a set of Australian uniform trousers turned civilian. Whatever useful bits and pieces anybody had went to equip the men who would try to survive the perils outside the wire.

With nothing but time to spend, however, the ingenious British fabricators pressed on. Buttons were removed from military clothing and replaced with civilian buttons carefully gleaned and hoarded.

The escapers could leave only a few at a time. Only three were scheduled to try the first break beneath the vaulting horse. More men were to follow if the tunnel stayed open and undiscovered by the guard force; it did not, as we will see.

Getting out through the tiny tunnel posed problems of its own. The escapers could not crawl through the dirt of that tiny tunnel wearing their street clothing. Those would have to be stuffed into bags and dragged behind them. To further complicate things, one prisoner would have to stay at the tunnel face while the horse was removed.

After it was replaced, there would be three prisoners crammed into the faithful horse, the last two escapers and somebody who would remain behind to close the trap door after them. That man would have to carefully sprinkle the camouflage sand as well. Even if the tunnel were never used again, discovery of it had to be delayed as long as possible.

The planning for flight after the escape also continued. Other escapers had thought to walk out to freedom. That course of action had the virtue of keeping to the woods and fields and away from congested areas. But it was also necessarily slow, and once their absence was discovered in the camp and the hue and cry went up, they still had many miles and days before them. Walking escapers were generally recaptured within a few days.

And so the attempt this time would use rapid transit, public transportation by rail, trading the risks of higher public exposure for a saving of many days of back roads and haystacks and scrounging for food. Two of the escapers had decided to head for Stettin, in north Germany, their ultimate goal sanctuary in neutral Sweden. Their planned route went through Frankfurt—then not an enchanting city—and the city of Kuestrin before heading north for Stettin and the sea.

Fleeing openly by rail also had the advantage of the cover afforded by the millions of foreign workers in Germany. Certain phrases the British escapers all learned: *ich bin auslaender* and *nicht verstehen*: "I am a foreigner" and "don't understand." Those two phrases, an uncomprehending look, and a good deal of luck would carry them a long way.

Eric Williams and Michael Codner would try to take the tunnel to freedom together. One of them spoke good French and could chatter away while his companion nodded brightly and tried to look like he understood. Since Germany was full of French workers, the pose would arouse no suspicion and add to their cover as *Fremdarbeiter*, foreign workers.

The tunnel progressed. There had been one major crisis along the way, what everybody feared most: a cave-in. A prisoner named John had been at the tunnel face, almost at the end of his shift, when a hole suddenly appeared on top of the ground. Another prisoner, Nigel, alertly fell on top of the hole, covering it with his body and pretending that he had hurt his leg. Prisoners called down the hole from the entrance, but there was no answer. As a couple of prisoners ran for a stretcher to carry Nigel, one prisoner crouched close to Nigel and again called for John down the hole.

There was still no answer.

They tried again, and this time Nigel cautiously moved enough to reveal a hole down into the tunnel, a gap about the size of a man's arm. Another call . . . and this time a faint answer.

"I have a cave-in," John said, "but I can clear it." He did, and it was the only major danger of the long days of digging.

But it is easy to imagine the long minutes while John fought that choking, clogging sand. The effort of groping for safety in primeval darkness, scraping and clogging at shifting sand, afraid of another sand-fall, had to have been terrifying. Then, when the night came for the break itself, it went as smoothly as they could wish: no cave-in, no alarm, no baying dogs, just free air and a chance to leave their prison far behind them. On the night of the breakout, the rest of the prisoners staged a carefully orchestrated demonstration involving much singing and shouting, the blare of musical instruments, even banging on the sides of the huts. It worked. Everybody's attention was riveted on the racket at the huts, and so the escapers' breakthrough from the tunnel and run for the shelter of the nearby woods went unnoticed.

The escapers were clear; no alarm, no dogs. They quickly changed into their civilian clothing and headed for the local rail-road station. Peter and John bought railroad tickets to Frankfurt and settled down to wait for the train. It was late, of course, as trains often were in the Third Reich at this time . . . when they came at all, that is.

Ollie Philpot elected to travel alone, also by train. He magically became a Norwegian margarine-maker, his goal also Sweden, via the North Sea city of Danzig. From Danzig he got passage on a ship, and within a week of arriving in Danzig reached neutral Sweden. It was a piece of luck to be sure, but it owed much to Philpot's coolness and masterful planning.

For by escape time, the endless Allied bomber offensive was gnawing deeply into the economic life of Germany. The Americans came by day, the RAF raided by night, and the huge tonnage of bombs not only tore great gaps in the German industrial machine and cut highways and railroads and streetcar lines but also ruined the sleep and efficiency of the German labor force. In addition, it helped produce weary crowds at most train stations, crowds into which escaping prisoners might hope to vanish.

There were some iffy moments. With only moments to go before Peter and John's first train, Peter almost ran into the prison doctor, a captain with whom he had spoken every day during a week in the hospital. But their luck was in: Peter had shaved his beard in preparation for the escape and had the presence of mind to bend over and fiddle with his attaché case. The doctor passed within two feet of Peter without a flicker of recognition. Peter and Michael waited on pins and needles, expecting the escape to be discovered momentarily. All remained quiet. That night their beds were filled by a couple of ghosts until, around midnight, the tunnel exit was finally found. There followed an extended *appell*, with much uncooperative foot-dragging by the prisoners.

As the endless inquisition dragged on, those prisoners not still in ranks ended up in a disorderly mass chasing a rugby ball. The "game" got wilder and wilder until at last an RAF wing commander kicked the ball directly at the prison staff conducting the inquisition in the midst of the exercise ground. A mass rush for the ball followed, and in the process, the inquisitors' table was "accidentally" knocked over, and their boxes of files scattered across the dirt.

The Germans now herded everybody inside and locked the doors. Still, it was 2:00 p.m. before they could finally learn who was missing, and Peter and Michael had been given some more priceless time. They carried on traveling north, staying in cheap hotels and eating tasteless meals in cheap restaurants. The French worker masquerade continued to prove itself.

There were moments of danger. Once, when a policeman came too close for comfort, Michael broke into a stream of French, while Peter simply sat and tried to look fascinated. Later he asked Michael what he had said: "I told you all about a letter I'd had from Tante Annette who said that she'd been in bed with bronchitis and that my sister Marie was having another baby."

Peter, who had contributed to the deception by looking deeply interested, pronounced the deception worth a beer, which they had forthwith. They were quickly gaining expertise in this art of escape.

In Stettin, they managed to make contact with real Frenchmen who worked for the Germans but cordially detested them as well. With their help, Michael and Peter got aboard a Swedish ship and ended up in that staunchly neutral nation. There they vegetated for almost seven weeks, eager to see England but unable to get there until a British aircraft landed and places were found for them.

It was as well they left when they did. Apparently on the night before they left Sweden they had crashed what they called a "wizard" party, which turned out to be some sort of official reception at the German embassy. There had apparently been considerable breakage of glass during the festivities, which also saw the disappearance of a large Nazi flag.

Still hung over, they got a telephone call with the wonderful news that they would fly out that very day. They were also directed, however, to return the flag. What had they done with it, said the voice on the phone, and Peter said the first thing that came into his head: "We burned it," while looking directly at Michael trying to fold the purloined banner. The officer on the phone was not fooled and his response was classic British military: "Hide it—wrap it round your arse if necessary. But if you let . . . anyone . . . catch a glimpse of it, I'll have your balls. Is that understood?"

Late that night they were back in England. So was the flag.

CHAPTER THREE

The *Ruth-Lee*

THE JAPANESE FORCED SOME SEVENTY THOUSAND AMERICAN and Filipino prisoners to march for their lives in April of 1942. One out of every seven didn't make it, dying of hunger, thirst, disease, brutality, or downright murder. Captain Damon Gause vowed he wouldn't be one of the dead.

Gause was born in Jefferson, Georgia, a bucolic backwater about a mile north of Atlanta in the hill country. He was a bright young man but not particularly interested in schoolwork. During his one year at the University of Georgia, he spent much of his time at an airfield just outside the university town of Athens, learning to fly. Not satisfied with rural life, he later did two hitches in the Coast Guard, a tour in Panama with the army, and some time in the Columbia oil fields with Texaco. Finally, he went to work for the Civil Aeronautics Administration.

When World War II began in Europe, Gause joined the Army Air Corps and became a pilot in the 27th Bombardment Group, then stationed in Savannah. When he was notified that he would be leaving for the Philippines in a month, he eloped with Ruth Evans, but by mid-November 1941 he was fighting sea sickness aboard the grandly appointed SS *President Coolidge*, a luxury liner commandeered for military transportation. While the *Coolidge* took on food and other supplies in Pearl Harbor, Gause and some buddies took in Diamond Head and Waikiki Beach.

The *Coolidge* arrived in Manilla on November 27. In the still-peaceful days that followed, Gause went sightseeing and did some Christmas shopping. General MacArthur, commanding in the Philippines, was sure that war was coming, but he expected the Japanese attack in the Philippines to come in about four months.

"Air raid at Pearl Harbor! This is no drill!" Even as important as this message was, nobody bothered to alert MacArthur in his penthouse at the Manilla Hotel. He found out a half-hour later, and only then because one of his soldiers picked up a radio news bulletin all the way from California. Gause got the news over breakfast at the Officers' Club and fell to gathering commo equipment as he had been ordered. Then the first bombs began to fall, leveling nearly every building in sight. In the midst of this chaos, Gause still found time to reassure his mother by radiogram: "Am alive and giving them hell."

The Japanese raids went on for days, destroying the Air Force on the ground, among other disasters. Only a single fighter—a P-40—was lost in a dogfight. There was worse on the way. The Hawaiian Islands had taken a similar battering, but the Philippines were about to be invaded. When the Japanese began to come ashore, Gause and many other men were ordered to the relative safety of Baguio, out on the Bataan Peninsula. Still, New Year's Eve found Gause and many others celebrating back in the Empire Room of the Manilla Hotel.

The Japanese were expected . . . within a few hours, so . . . the bars were well patronized. I thought of the boys digging in on Bataan. They would never believe that I celebrated the approach of a New Year—and the Japanese Army—from a front-row seat in the doomed city. Everybody danced that night, young and old. Against the distant rumbling of big guns, the music was loud and occasionally off-key. People were drinking too much . . . there was much loud talking and raucous laughter as people tried to forget.

And he finished his comments with a prophetic sentence: "We were commemorating the passing of an era as well as a year."

His date that momentous night was Rita Garcia, a twenty-something beauty he had found bleeding in the street during one of the early Japanese attacks. They partied until 3:30 a.m., when he dropped Rita off and headed for Bataan.

Gause was on the last convoy out of doomed Manilla. He joined other airmen defending a line from the mountains to the sea with little more weaponry that some air-cooled machine guns, intended for aircraft that had never arrived. Mounts had to be improvised, like the old carriage on which Private James Oestricher manage to hang two machine guns, camouflaged with a dummy haystack. He nailed two dive-bombers from his crude position—but then, like so many others, Oestricher, as soldiers say, bought the farm.

Gause survived a massive Japanese assault in early January, but then came a lull in which the Americans survived on monkeys and whatever else they could scrounge. Early in April, the Americans had to fall back, the roads behind them littered with gear and supplies, even souvenirs taken from Japanese dead. There were close calls, some of which Gause recorded in his journal, hand-cut paper held together with cardboard and copper wire.

Later Gause recalled being beneath heavy foliage with no working weapons. Sgt. Baker wondered out loud how they would defend themselves, even as they heard bayonets being spiked into the brush along a river bank. One bayonet almost struck Gause.

But the Japanese missed them. Gause and Baker dodged patrols hunting them and even slept in a Japanese camp next to an enemy soldier before they waded into the neutral waters of Manilla Bay one night. Gause was still free, but he never saw Sergeant Baker again.

Once ashore, Gause met a Filipino who told him the Japanese were everywhere. They were. Gause soon stumbled into two of them, who robbed him of all he carried and then prodded him to an enclosure already containing some three hundred other Americans. Watching Japanese soldiers torturing civilians just for sport quickly convinced Gause that the camp was no place for him. And so, when one of the Japanese became a little careless, Gause killed him with his own knife.

Gause ran through the brush toward Manilla Bay with a pack of Japanese soldiers about thirty seconds behind him, but he had enough of a lead to let him make the first hundred yards of a three-mile swim. In spite of a shower of poorly aimed Japanese bullets, he made it out to an abandoned steamer. After a brief rest, he cut loose a lifeboat and rowed the rest of the way to the fortress island of Corregidor.

Gause crawled ashore around sundown and simply fell asleep. He woke up thirty-six hours later looking at a high school friend, Millie Dalton. He was in Malinta Tunnel, deep in the heart of Corregidor, then headquarters for what was left of the American presence in the Philippines.

After a little more rest, he assumed joint command of a machine gun company facing across the bay to Bataan. The Japanese artillery hammered them regularly, directed by an observation balloon moored just out of range. The artillery was bad enough; things were about to get worse.

The 29th of April was the emperor's birthday. The Japanese celebrated by mounting a full-scale assault the next morning. Gause decided not to wait for the inevitable and left ahead of the invaders with Filipino Lieutenant Alberto Arranzaso. Hiding during the day, they came upon an old outrigger that could carry them across the bay. The little craft also attracted unwanted attention from the air, this time Filipino aircraft. The two men were repeatedly strafed by their own people, and Arranzaso was mortally wounded. He gave Gause his money belt before he died, along with the assurance that "I'm certain my mother is alive and can help you."

Gause and his little outrigger made it as far as a tiny island that night. He collapsed on the beach, exhausted, only to be awakened by a kick in the darkness. It was a Japanese patrol, but it did not stop moving forward, probably assuming Gause was just another dead American washed up out of Manilla Bay.

Gause was worn out, and his clothing was reduced to a pair of faded blue denim shorts and a weary sleeveless shirt. Nevertheless, he set out to find Arranzaso's mother. He stole from Japanese camps as he moved, feasting on such peculiar treats as a melon washed down with beer. Scrounging bird eggs as he went, dodging Japanese patrols, he met, of all people, the eleven-year-old brother of his Manilla date, Rita Garcia.

He soon met Rita, who found him shelter in a shed used to store rice. She also admitted she had not mailed a letter he had asked her to send, a letter to Gause's wife.

In a nearby town, some three hundred Americans who had been forced to rebuild docks and bridges had rebelled. The Japanese reaction was to hang two officers for an entire morning by their broken arms, then stake them out for the ants and other insects.

So Gause decided on the unthinkable, escape all the way to Australia, three thousand miles by open boat. First, however, there was the matter of finding Lieutenant Arranzaso's mother; he had promised to see her, and there was the possibility that she could help. Rita went with Gause; she wanted to go with him, and she was of immense help communicating with the Filipinos. They were eager to help, and poor and hungry as they were, they never failed to share whatever little food they had. Rita also schooled Gause in rudimentary Tagalog, in case they got separated.

By the end of May, Rita found Arranzaso's mother, living in poverty in a shanty next to her own fine house . . . now occupied by the Japanese. Her son's money belt would help to relieve her want, and now Gause and Rita could move on, this time to a hideout on the beach. Rita's relatives scrounged a small boat for them, and they moved on across Manilla Bay.

Gause dared to go into Manilla with a Spanish official. The two even went night-clubbing with some Japanese officers, Gause covering his identity by a pretense of drunkenness and some mumbled words of his very limited Spanish.

Gause had heard of a mysterious American known as "Colonel Wells" and went in search of him. Wells said yes, he had a connection to U.S. Naval Intelligence, and so the matter rested, until the arrival of army captain Lloyd Osborne, coming in response to a note sent him by Gause. The introduction of Osborne to Wells did not go well, with Osborne recoiling in repugnance. He later told Gause that Wells was hostile, arrested by Osborne before the war. He had killed a guard, escaped, and was a danger to them if he had any weapons. As Gause told the tale later: the wind moved some netting just above him when he saw someone in the far corner of the room.

The intruder was Colonel Wells, and he was holding a revolver in his right hand. Gause threw himself at Wells's legs and knocked him down. The two men wrestled for the revolver and the weapon fired, wounding Wells in the stomach. It was over. Wells, as Gause learned later, was a German agent, even if he sounded American and had studied at Yale. Just now, he was also *kaput*.

Gause was now even more determined to get out of the Philippines. He asked Osborne to come to Australia with him, and Rita's connections found them a twenty-foot skiff with a cranky little engine Gause named the "Little Swede" for reasons now lost in the mists of time. Gause now told Rita she could not go along, a judgment that seems cruel in retrospect, but at least would protect her from all the hazards of the voyage to come.

He sailed with Osborne to Tividad, where the local natives, helpful as always, helped them tune their engine, improvise mast and sails, and patch their boat, originally somewhat grandly named *Empress of Mindoro* but now rechristened *Ruth-Lee*, in honor of their wives. They provisioned *Ruth-Lee* from a lighthouse, tying up the sole Japanese guard and departing with his supplies and rising-sun flag.

Although the *Ruth-Lee* was—in their own words—"a patched-up derelict of questionable seaworthiness," she stayed afloat. The big worry was the Japanese fleet, both naval and merchant, like the ship that spotted them and signaled something to them unintelligible. Gause replied with the only Japanese words he knew: *banzai Nippon.* Apparently "long live Japan" was good enough, for the ship let them proceed.

And then there was the Little Swede to contend with. The rusting diesel engine they had coaxed back to life turned temperamental, refusing to start, leaving their makeshift mast and flour-sack sail as their only motive power. They let a light wind push them across heavy seas toward Culion Island, then the largest leper colony in the world. The island governor was a Spaniard, whose authority had been tacitly approved by Japanese forces across Coron Bay, even though the day-to-day work of the place was supervised by American doctors.

"The leper city was an inviting little place," Gause remembered, "except for the disease connected with it. Smart white house and business structures, resembling tombstones from a distance, dominated by a large hospital building stuck up from the terraced hill. I didn't think of the resemblance then, and that was fortunate, because I was leery as it was about bouncing into a leper colony."

The Japanese seldom visited the colony. The Culion Island governor said he would help Gause and Osborne with the repair and reprovisioning of their little boat. He asked only that *Ruth-Lee* be hidden in a nearby creek. If the fugitives were spotted by the Japanese, he said, everybody in the colony might be killed.

The governor kept his word. Both the engine and a broken propeller shaft were quickly repaired, and the colony even found a compass for the *Ruth-Lee*. And then it was back to the high seas again, going aground once, perpetually wrestling with their balky little engine, weathering monsoon rains, often forced to pitch their makeshift mast and rely on their flour-sack sail.

The Japanese were everywhere. Gause and Osborne crept by a Japanese garrison at Puerto Princesa, sporting a Japanese flag and accompanied by a shark they named Butch, whom they later turned into supper. Once they pushed into a lagoon covered with overhanging branches, eluding a Japanese launch.

In time the Little Swede called it quits again. This time repairs were made by a young American, scion of local plantation owners, and a former engineering student at the University of Chicago. That got them going once more, this time for Borneo, into the teeth of a typhoon's fifteen-foot waves and seventy-mile-per-hour winds. When the storm's force abated from one direction, it shifted to another. It looked like the end.

The *Ruth-Lee* was leaking badly now. Osborne bailed perpetually; as Gause put it, "It was bail or sink, and that might be swim or sink," even as torrents hit them again and again.

It got worse. The extra wood and coconuts had been washed overboard, the front of the cabin was smashed, and the boat was leaking badly. Now the rudder broke and had to be operated by moving it with two bamboo poles. They badly needed some good luck, and miraculously, they got it: a small uncharted island just ahead of their tiny boat. They managed to come about and land on the lee side of the island, a place called Cagayan Sulu. It was a heaven-sent refuge for the weary men while the storm passed over.

They put back to sea, but a few days later came the "gurgling noise," a noise like a giant whirlpool, a frightening sound. They were almost relieved when it turned out to be a Japanese submarine. The crew ignored them, however, or really didn't see them, being preoccupied with repairing something to do with their deck gun to bother with an insignificant little skiff.

Two days later, Gause and Osborne made landfall at British North Borneo. After spending a couple of days hung up on a reef, they managed to get into Darvel Bay and the down-at-the-heels village there. But there were also four natives wearing the Crown's uniform who replenished the men's dwindling supplies.

From there it was into Makassar Strait. There were lots of Japanese craft there too, but that turned out to be to their advantage. Their Japanese flag made them look like all the other small craft. From the strait they turned down the west coast of the Celebes, sometimes going ashore for fresh water. And here, along the way, they acquired another traveling companion. This time, he saw a fin traveling along next to the boat and heard banging beneath them. Before he knew it, a sailfish arced out of the water above them and soon disappeared.

They were filthy by now, a quality that might have helped them as they lustily cheered three passing Japanese warships; they were masters of the seafaring trade and very confident—until they stopped at a coastal village in the Timor Sea. They hoisted their Japanese flag and went ashore, but they had been careless, for this little village had a Japanese garrison.

Osborne and I did an abrupt about-face and moved toward the beach, not at a run, but at the quickest quick-time I ever made. Once past the houses we broke into a run and when we emerged on the beach who should be standing before us but a sentry with a gun on his shoulder.

He used it, too. The sentry opened fire on little *Ruth-Lee* as the men sailed away, but the Japanese was a lousy shot and the Americans quickly opened the range. They had some 2,500 miles of their 3,200-mile voyage behind them, but there was still danger everywhere. Gause put it plainly, "The Japanese were thicker in these waters than buzzards around a battlefield." There was much hiding to do, like the day *Ruth-Lee* spent camouflaged in a lagoon directly beneath the glide path of a Japanese airfield.

By now they were running their little diesel engine on coconut oil, down from their usual kerosene, and both wondered how long the Little Swede would last. They spent much of their time evading Japanese patrol boats, and once were attacked by an enemy fighter that made two strafing passes at them . . . but then flew away without finishing the job.

At last came the really important landfall, Australia. They had trouble finding water along that inhospitable coast, and the Little Swede sounded ready to quit, but then, six days after they first saw the Land Down Under, an Australian patrol boat warily approached this derelict and her two filthy crew members. The long voyage was over at last. The next day they were taken to see the Allied commander. Gause was barefoot, his feet so sunburned he could not tolerate shoes. Let Gause tell the end of the tale:

> *The palatial hotel where General MacArthur was quartered was bustling with activity, but everything stopped and many mouths dropped when Osborne and I walked into the pillared lobby. I slithered across the marble floor in my bare feet. I was burned nearly black but ecstatically happy. . . . I was announced, stepped into the general's office, walked to his desk, and saluted.*
>
> *"Sir, Lieutenant Gause reports for duty from Corregidor!"*
>
> *The general rose, peered intently at this ragged apparition, and returned the salute. He spoke: "Well I'll be damned!"*

They were home.

Both Gause and Osborne received the Distinguished Service Cross, and Gause was assigned to what most men would have considered prime duty, touring America promoting war bond sales with his wife, Ruth. But by the next summer he was getting restless and requested a return to active duty. After leave to visit his wife and new son—born on the second anniversary of Pearl Harbor—he got his wish and returned to the wars.

Sadly, his return to active duty was short. After flying five daylight missions over Germany early in 1944, he went up to test fly a new model of the P-47 fighter.

He did not survive the crash.

CHAPTER FOUR

After Midnight

*Misery acquaints a man with strange bedfellows. I will here
shroud till the dregs of the storm be past.*
            —THE TEMPEST, ACT 2, SCENE 2

THEY WERE A STRANGE LOT TO BE SURE: AN ANTI-SEMITIC
carpenter who had married an Orthodox Jew, the carpenter's
brothel-keeping mother, and two German soldiers. Yet for their
own reasons, some noble, some not, these four nondescript indi-
viduals helped six-year-old Johna Christiansen and many other
Danish Jews escape all but certain death in the Holocaust. And
it all began in the early hours of October 7, 1943, forty-two
months after the Nazis first marched into Copenhagen.

Denmark had been occupied in a matter of hours. The first alert
from the frontier came in at 4:00 a.m. that spring morning, and the
king was facing German troops on the Palace Square in Copenhagen within less than an hour. By seven that morning, Tuesday,
April 9, 1940, the king had ordered Danish troops to stand down.
In return, the Germans promised not to interfere with Danish ter-
ritorial integrity or political independence. Only a year earlier, the
Danes had signed a nonaggression pact with Germany.

The surrender was peaceful, but most Danes soon began practicing passive resistance, simply "cold-shouldering" the occupying Germans in every way they could. In one instance, after a German soldier boarded a streetcar in downtown Copenhagen, everyone else moved to the platforms outside until he left. German censorship of the Danish press began in June 1940, followed six months later by the surrender of Denmark's submarines for use against the Allies. The arrest of Danish Communists and severance of diplomatic ties to Soviet Russia soon followed.

The Danish Resistance began with students who published underground newspapers and committed "individual acts of sabotage." The first Resistance group, known as the "Churchill Club," organized in early 1942 at the Aalborg Cathedral School, at the start resembled a teenage street gang more than a paramilitary organization. Before they were arrested in May 1942, however, the seven Churchillians had conducted over twenty operations, most notably burning an entire supply train.

When King Christian simply responded "my utmost thanks" to an effusive, lengthy birthday greeting from Hitler in the fall of 1942, the sauerkraut hit the fan. Hitler immediately replaced the diplomat in charge of Denmark by appointing the aggressive SS General Werner Best.

Danish Resistance accelerated in a wave of strikes and sabotage beginning in April 1943. This culminated in a July 28 strike at Odense, in which a German minesweeper was destroyed. Less than a month later, on August 24, the Resistance destroyed German barracks under construction northwest of Copenhagen at Frederiksberg, prompting the Germans to proclaim a state of emergency. The proclamation restricted all meetings and directed the Danes to surrender all arms and explosives under penalty of death.

The Danish government responded that it had no intention of complying with the ultimatum, prompting the German forces to attack selected Danish army garrisons nationwide on August 28. The Danish navy scuttled twenty-nine ships and moved thirteen others to Sweden.

German Commander Herman Von Hanneken declared the Danish government "superseded" on August 29. That evening, German diplomat George F. Duckwitz recorded his view of the consequences in his diary: "Four years of hard work is for naught—because of stupidity and unreasonableness. Now the inhabitants of the last country in Europe will hate us from the bottom of their hearts. It is very difficult to be a German."

Duckwitz, the scion of a prominent Bremen merchant family, had arrived in Copenhagen sixteen years earlier to represent Kaffee Haag, a sort of German Starbucks. Three years later, in 1932, Duckwitz joined the Nazi Party. One historian has maintained that Duckwitz was also in the SS, although another historian stated in 2002 that no archival evidence supports this. That said, Duckwitz had a close relationship with SS General Best, initiated by Best, probably prompted largely by the wide circle of Danish contacts that Duckwitz enjoyed.

When Best sent a cable to Berlin recommending that the Danish Jews be temporarily placed in Copenhagen work camps and then deported, Duckwitz objected and asked for a transfer but was convinced by Danish friends to stay.

Perhaps this was no coincidence. Earlier in his career, Duckwitz had been in the Abwehr, the very intelligence unit within the German high command that later participated in efforts to assassinate Hitler.

But now, years before the attempts to kill *Der Fuhrer*, Duckwitz took action. On September 21, 1943, he traveled to

Stockholm, where he met with the Swedish prime minister to explain the dangers facing the Danish Jews. In the days to come, Duckwitz recruited others, notably high officials of the German Admiralty in Denmark as well as two harbormasters, to do as much as possible to derail the deportation, on practical as well as humanitarian grounds.

One of the two harbormasters, Friedrich Wilhelm Lubke, conspired with the captain of the German hospital ship *Monte Rosa*, who pretended that the ship's engines had been seriously damaged, requiring repairs and forcing the deployment of two German ships. Thanks to Duckwitz and others, those ships did not carry a single Jew to deportation.

Despite all this, Best informed Duckwitz on September 28 that the Jews were to be picked up and deported on the night of October 1–2. Duckwitz immediately informed Hans Hedroft, future Danish prime minister, who helped commandeer police cars and notified as many leaders of the Copenhagen Jewish community as he could find. Some were astonished. Carl Bernard Henriques spoke for many when he told the messenger who brought the news, "You're lying." After lengthy discussions, Henriques and the other Jewish leaders decided that something had to be done.

And although the story of King Christian wearing a Star of David to protest German demands for anti-Jewish legislation is said to be a myth, Danish Jews were not harassed until August 1943, when the Resistance became most active. On the other hand, German Jews were denied asylum in Denmark due to highly restrictive immigration rules that were applied to Jews and non-Jews alike.

There was one notable exception. Several Danish women's organizations combined efforts to help several hundred German-Jewish children immigrate to Denmark with the hope of saving their lives and eventually reuniting them with their parents in Palestine.

Young Johna had endured taunts from a young age—for being Jewish, to be sure, but mostly due to a five-pointed stub where her left hand should have been. And the glasses she had to wear didn't help. Her parents, Paul and Margit, had not married until she was three. Margit's Orthodox Jewish parents initially objected to the marriage on religious grounds but finally relented.

Her father, Paul, had become friends with several German soldiers since the Nazi occupation of Sweden quietly began in April 1940. His reasons became apparent later: He was part of the Danish Resistance. When word spread in late September 1943 that the Jewish population in Denmark, then consisting of about seven thousand, was about to be deported to the long-rumored death camps spread around Europe, a quiet revolt began.

About two months earlier, the peaceful occupation had suddenly become a noisy and aggressive affair complete with tanks rumbling through the streets and fighter planes roaring through the skies above. When she prepared her memoirs many years later, Johna remembered that day distinctly:

Behind the tanks came the soldiers. They wore brownish-green uniforms and looked like a huge army of ants with steel helmets covering their large round heads. They had rifles hanging from their shoulders and shiny boots that were nearly as tall as we were. They marched like wind-up toys, kicking their legs high in the air, their boots drumming the ground.

As we watched, three soldiers approached the sidewalk, shoving their way through the people. One bulky solder forced his way up to the fruit stand outside the grocery store and grabbed all the grapes he could hold in his hands. Laughing, he tossed the fresh fruit to other German soldiers who were not

marching. Some [soldiers] missed the toss and the grapes fell to
the ground to be instantly crushed by the shiny boots stamping
down the street. I knew that they had not paid for the produce.

From behind her, someone in the crowd began to discuss the
danger the Jews were now in. Although only six, she recognized
the kinds of whispers used "when women talked about neighbors
who weren't there." But there was something new:

Most of our neighbors weren't Jewish, but until that moment,
I never thought my being a Jew was of interest to anyone. The
synagogue and my Jewish grandparents were one part of my
life, and my Danish family and neighbors were another. That
was just how life was, and it had not been worth noticing
the difference. My father told me I was half-Danish, the good
half, the Viking half. My mother and her father told me I was
all Jewish. Rather than be confused, I simply hadn't thought
about it at all.

When Johna returned to her apartment with the news,
that day in late September 1943, her father announced that
the Germans would not bother his wife and child since they
weren't Jews anymore. Johna asked how this could be, but Paul
just ignored her question and soon left for an evening meeting
with his Nazi friends.

Johna and her mother soon learned that the German army
had broken into a synagogue across town, rifling through the cabinets and desks in the rabbi's office to find the addresses of everyone who attended. And Paul discovered that his contacts in the
Nazi Party had new policies that excluded Paul because he had a
handicapped Jewish child. This complicated Paul's other life away
from home in ways that Johna would only learn about years later.

His friend Steen Larsen also lived in their building. Larsen, a mason by trade, kept pure white messenger pigeons (really, rock doves) on the roof. From time to time, Johna saw Mr. Larsen tie thin strips of papers to the bird's ankles before shooing them into flight. The messages were secret, her father told her.

A few days after the tanks came into Copenhagen, her father joined the Resistance—and Johna had two secrets to keep. That September her father began inviting his friends to join him. These men included the architect Thor Pehrrsen and handsome, perpetually smiling Erik Olsen, who wore starched white shirts and expensive suits with lots of money in his pockets, as becoming a professional thief and smuggler. Erik was very somber that first night; he warned everyone present of the German warning that any Dane who refused to give up his weapons would be shot without a trial.

Paul had never before said a kind word about his Jewish in-laws, the Pressmans, whom Johna knew by their Yiddish names Bubbe (grandmother) and Zayde (grandfather). In fact, he had ridiculed their Orthodox Jewish ways, often to their faces. But now Paul vowed that he would not allow them to be harmed. That very night Johna noticed a dark metal object stuffed in the waist of his pants.

The black-helmeted Gestapo soon became more aggressive than ever, shoving pedestrians into lines along the sidewalks, just to show who was boss. Johna's parents began hiding the extra money Paul made selling homemade vodka, and the few anti-Semites in Johna's school became bolder. Although one such classmate called Johna "a blind, crippled, one-armed stupid Jew" on the playground, many others warned Johna and her parents about certain Danes who had become informers.

Neither the British nor Americans started the gunfire that early fall in Copenhagen. It was the Resistance, which began open hostilities by inciting a riot in the shipyards. Johna's father, Paul, had been part of it—just before running home to hurry his own small family into the apartment basement and then rejoining the fight. While there, Johna and her best friend Hanne drew a picture of Hanne's prized red umbrella on the basement wall, just before Hanne quietly said that they couldn't be friends anymore because Johna was a Jew.

She stayed home that week—in the days before Rosh Hashanah, the Jewish New Year, which began on Friday, September 30, 1943. Although Paul seldom escorted Johna and her mother, Margit, to the synagogue, on the morning of September 29 he did so, bringing along his friend Erik for extra protection. Along the way, they stopped at a cigar store, just as German soldiers nailed a board across the windows, chalked with the word "JUDEN" while motioning them away with rifles.

And so it came to be that in an early service, the day before Rosh Hashanah, Rabbi Marcus Melchior warned Johna, her family, and hundreds of others of impending danger: "I have important news."

That morning Rabbi Melchior cancelled services and warned his congregation to go into hiding, thanks to a German diplomat who opposed Hitler's policies against the Jews. "Everyone, please listen," Johna remembered Melchior saying years later. "There will be no service today! The Germans are planning to round up all the Jews in Denmark tomorrow and ship them to work camps." As the congregation rushed from the synagogue, young Johna asked her mother, "Am I a Jew again?" only to be told she must keep a third secret. "We are Danes, remember?"

When he learned of this, Johna's father crammed his in-laws, the Pressmanns, and his own small family into Erik's car for the quick drive to the Christensen apartment, knowing they couldn't stay there long. Paul then went for help to his mother's place, the Café Absalon.

The Absalon occupied the first two floors of a four-story commercial building. It wasn't much to look at but had certain amenities that attracted many of the German soldiers stationed in Copenhagen. Years later, Johna realized that her stout, cigar-smoking grandmother Pauline ran a brothel. One of the German patrons was Alfred, a German officer who was devoted to Nazism yet had a Jewish girlfriend named Emma. Paul had introduced the couple without telling Alfred about her religious background. This was no coincidence.

Alfred arrived that Thursday evening wearing a full dress uniform with a second German officer who strongly resembled him named Carl. "They looked like twin toy soldiers," Johna recalled years later. Alfred also had important news: "Hitler's in a rage, blaming the Danish Jews for all the sabotage that's been happening lately, for blowing up the railroad tracks and train cars," he explained in hushed tones. And that is how it began.

"That's nuts!" Paul exploded. "That's the kind of thinking that made me stop going to those Nazi meetings." Then, just as quickly he stopped himself, then he laughed. "Next thing we know" he said in a jovial way, "they'll be arresting Danes who are married to Jews."

"Some Danes involved with Jews have already been arrested, Paul," Alfred said.

During the long silence that followed, Johna watched her father's hands tremble. Finally, Alfred, the German officer, broke the silence. "Let's just you and me work together to help Emma and your family . . . agreed?" Paul nodded his assent as Alfred became angry. "I do not choose to hurt innocent human beings," he murmured.

"Perhaps we should not get so involved with helping Paul's family," the new stranger, Carl, said in the darkness.

Alfred answered: "These are not normal times, Carl. I need him to help Emma and Paul is willing to help his wife's family and needs help with that. Understand?" The stranger said nothing.

Paul became very quiet and then asked in a whisper "Do you know a hiding place for my wife's parents?"

"All right, Paul," Alfred said at last. "I will give you an address and a key to a house that a family has already vacated. It will not be searched again. I'll make sure of that."

And so the deal was done.

While Johna and her father were at the Absalon, Johna's mother and her parents, the Pressmanns, watched German soldiers begin roaming the Copenhagen streets in search of Jews. After some resistance, Johna's grandfather shaved the beard so important to many Orthodox Jewish men then and now.

Soon they were climbing into Erik's car for the trip to Alfred's hiding place in Gilleleje, a fishing village dating from the sixteenth century some thirty-nine miles north of Copenhagen. After they went inside, as Paul tried to help his father-in-law open one of their many suitcases, pots and pans fell onto the floor with a bang. After some yelling and screaming, Paul agreed to bring back only the types of food that Orthodox Jews could cook and eat. Before he left, however, Paul hung a tapestry in the window bearing the image of a Danish saint facing into the darkness to deflect suspicions, over Zayde's shouts of "blasphemy."

This was just the beginning. Johna's mother fled their apartment to live in a hospital with other Jews in hiding. And since they would soon be on the run, Paul insisted that when Margit left the hospital, the new baby in her stomach couldn't come.

Early the next morning, Johna, her father, his friend Erik, and several others from the Resistance watched a German soldier pull a car full of bloodied bodies down a street near the apartment. "Weren't those people sleeping?" six-year-old Johna asked. Looking over his shoulder, Paul murmured "Ja, they were sleeping." Within a few years, Johna knew better.

The next evening, Johna and her father went to a pawnshop Paul's brother Orla owned, as she recalled some fifty-seven years later:

> *At Uncle Orla's pawnshop [her father] had his own key and unlocked the entrance. Inside were lots of knick-knacks, old lamps, oriental rugs, fancy blue plates, and dolls on display, and all manner and kinds of things filled the many cupboards that stood around the walls. Uncle Orla was working at the counter near the back of the room. He looked up as we came in and waved at [father.] As we walked toward him, he pushed aside a green curtain that covered the entrance to another room. Inside were several men who stood beside a locked jewelry counter. Several others sat on an orange, three-pillow couch.*

Her father's friend, the architect Thor Pehrrsen, and several other men were preparing fake identification papers in the back of the store, even as the Germans were arresting every Jew they could find on the street just a few yards away. Despite this, Johna was asleep within minutes.

With the dawn came a new job for the Resistance. Johna and her father went out that day at about noon. They followed a large plume of black smoke to the railroad yard, where Paul smiled slightly before posing Johna in front of overturned boxcars and engines, "scattered on top of twisted tracks and broken railroad ties. Fire still licked at the sky, and thick smoke drifted over the warehouses and other buildings, filling the air with a bad smell." But, of course, it wasn't a bad smell so far as the Resistance was concerned.

Later, at the harbor, they learned that at least one of the ships there held Jews being transported to work camps. While there, Alfred (the German officer) peddled up on a bicycle. Alfred's passenger, a skinny redhead named Myra, smiled and kissed Johna's father for a long, long time, before she began telling him about the doings at the most recent Nazi meeting in town. And Alfred and Paul still needed money to get Alfred's girlfriend Emma, Paul's in-laws, and Paul's family out of Denmark.

When the Germans began arresting the Danish police, her father taught Johna a new skill. With some practice, she could quietly run to a large cedar chest and hide inside beneath some sheets. One floor above the Christensen apartment, Mrs. Johnson, also a Jew, hid her elderly parents in a back closet. And before long, the Germans arrived at the Christensen apartment building trying unsuccessfully to find them.

As those first few days of October passed, Johna's father became more active in the Resistance, even as the Germans became more aggressive. Years later, Johna described the day she was walking with her father to meet someone in Fredens Park on a rainy afternoon:

Suddenly, a loud bang came from within the park, startling me. Father dragged me behind a bush and put his hand gently over my mouth.

Across the way from where we hid, German soldiers were tying three men to fence posts. After they were done, the soldiers dipped handkerchiefs in the water puddles and slapped them on the men's chests. The men tied to the posts all screamed something, but it was drowned out by the laughter of the soldiers. As I watched this strange scene, one of the officers lifted his pistol and fired shots through each one of the handkerchiefs. Blood gushed from the men as they doubled up and slumped away from the cords that held them to the posts.

Just then Father jerked me upright. He swept me up into his arms and began to run out of the park, keeping low behind the bushes. He rushed to a nearby apartment foyer and we hid behind a staircase. Then I heard a sob. I looked up and Father was crying. This frightened me so much I began to cry too.

Later, over a bottle of whiskey, her father explained to his friend Erik that he and Johna were in Fredens Park to meet the very men who had just been murdered. Those men had been her father's friends; that night, Paul was in no mood to tolerate informers.

The large neon light over the door at the Café Absalon was off the next evening when they arrived. A card in the window told patrons that the place was closed, but there was something blocking the door.

"Can you spare some coins for me today, Paul?" The question startled Johna, who glanced down at the ground to see a double amputee on a square skateboard glaring upward at her father. "No!" her father yelled, "F— off and move out of the way." The amputee was unafraid. "You think you are such a big man, but your little girl is a Jew. Who would like to know that, I wonder? All you have to do is give me a few coins and I won't tell the Germans anything." Johna went through the door, looked back through the window pane, and saw what to her was a strange thing.

Her father picked up the cripple, put his hand over the man's mouth, and carried him into the alley. She was terrified when her father and Erik came into the kitchen a few minutes later dripping with blood. Later that evening, she glanced out into the darkness, where she spotted a dark bloody lump on the edge of the shadows. Her grandmother told Johna that it was a butchered beef that would be brought in later. Mercifully, six-year-old Johna didn't connect the things she'd seen for many years.

Now the Germans began to search more intensely for the Jews. While at the Christensen apartment building, the Nazis poisoned Mr. Larsen's messenger pigeons nesting on the roof. And soon after that someone painted "Jud" on the Christiansen door. The time to leave Copenhagen had come.

The Christensen escape was carried out with the help of the Danish Resistance and sympathetic German soldiers, a few of whom were bribed. Of course, this was not the first time during the war that heroic efforts saved at least some European Jews. Nicholas Winton, a first-generation Englishman of German-Jewish parents and later called "the British Schindler," had arranged and financed the escape of nearly seven hundred mostly Jewish children from the Nazis. Beginning in March 1939, he personally arranged for six trains to carry refugee children from Prague, Czechoslovakia, to safety. The last such train, scheduled to depart Prague on September 1, 1939, had to be cancelled two days before the war started.

Those last children whom Winton tried to rescue virtually all died in concentration camps, but others escaped from Prague, as one Tom Weiss remembered years later. A German officer nearly detained the Weiss family, claiming, quite correctly, that their passports were forgeries. After the war began on September 3, Weiss and his family tried twice to cross from Italy into France by boat, and finally succeeded by railroad.

Yet, in a few instances, the Resistance in Europe took out Nazi monsters like Reinhard Heydrich, the most powerful SS official in the Third Reich after Heinrich Himmler. Heydrich has often been identified as the "architect" of the extermination the Nazis called the Final Solution, if such a bland term can possibly describe such vile cowardice.

He served as the "deputy Reich protector of Bohemia and Moravia." Heydrich, whom Hitler himself described as "the man with the iron heart," was blown out of his green Mercedes convertible on May 27, 1942, and died a few days later in mysterious circumstances. The exact cause of his death has been the subject of speculation ever since. One theory is that British intelligence provided toxin-laced grenades for the assassination, just in case he was not killed in the initial blast. Another theory, substantiated in part later by hospital staff, places Resistance sympathizers among the Heydrich medical team. Someone intentionally used the wrong blood type in Heydrich's transfusions to finish him off, or so the story goes.

But now for Johna's family and Emma: It all began on the evening of October 7, 1943. Alfred, the German officer who had offered to help Paul's extended family and Emma, his own Jewish girlfriend, followed through with all the arrangements. Emma had joined Paul's family and the Pressmanns, who had been retrieved from Gilleleje for the passage into Sweden. The Pressmanns and Emma were already waiting in Erik's car when Paul, Margit, and Johna jumped in.

Their next stop was a dairy farm near Elsinore (Heslinger), where Kronborg Castle, the setting for Shakespeare's *Hamlet*, guards the Oresund, the strait between Denmark and Sweden. As they left Erik's car and walked into the darkness, Johna's grandfather dropped and broke his most prized possession, a violin. Soon they were sitting in the open among some forty men, women, and children, all hiding from the Nazis.

The next night, Paul arranged for all forty refugees to move by ambulance to a nearby barn, where they listened to mice scamper through the hayloft. And on their final night in Elsinore, they all walked to the sea. Some carried suitcases but most carried bundles, often consisting only of pillowcases tied up with string, carrying everything they owned.

Small searchlights were used to quickly guide the refugees into small rowboats. Erik carried Johna to the rowboats. "I'm not coming with you, sweet Johna," he whispered. She never saw him again.

Thinking about the hours that followed fifty-seven years later, Johna couldn't decide whether she was more frightened braving ten-foot waves in a small rowboat that swirled in circle after circle, or climbing on a wobbly, slime-caked ladder into the fishing boat:

When it was my turn, Father untied the rope that held me to Mother. I stepped up on the first rung, grabbed the slippery ladder with my right hand and hooked the elbow of my short [crippled] arm inside the rope rung and held on. I was afraid to move, afraid I would not be able to hold on and climb at the same time without falling into the cold sea.

"Come on Johna, you can do it"

The ladder twisted and turned with each movement of the waves. My hand slid when I tried to raise myself and I lost my grip, leaving only my left elbow holding me to the ladder as my body slammed into the boat, I screamed.

"Shush!" Father said as he caught my legs in his firm grip, leaving me hanging upside down over the water. My glasses fell off my face and into the ocean. Carefully, balancing himself between the bobbing rowboat and the fishing boat, he turned me right-side up again.

There was no warning at all when the Germans began shooting at the helpless, unarmed refugees. One man was so distraught he jumped over the side. In those few seconds that seemed like hours, Alfred's girlfriend, Emma, was killed. And just as suddenly as it began, the Germans let them escape.

Some 7,220 Jews were saved that night. Johna's grandfather died several months later in Sweden, her grandmother returned to Copenhagen after the war, but Johna and her parents moved to the United States where her mother and father died within two years of each other in the early 1960s.

Johna eventually returned to Denmark, revisited the Copenhagen synagogue where she had learned her destiny years earlier, then crossed into Sweden to visit the Swedish nurse who had taken her family in for the duration of the war. In 1999, shortly before she completed her memoir, just three years before her death, Johna visited the Wailing Wall in Jerusalem, where her thoughts turned to her grandfather, her Zayde: "The Wall itself was like a magnet, binding together my Jewish heritage and all the survivors of the Holocaust. I wrote a note with the names of my deceased Jewish family and friends on it, and like thousands of pilgrims before me, I placed it in the crack of the wall."

Her grandfather would have said the names ascended into heaven.

And Johna eventually got her own red umbrella.

Chapter Five

Wish Me Luck as You Wave Me Good-Bye

Even after the German panzer spearheads smashed across the Polish border in 1939, there remained a few members of the British Parliament who still hesitated to plunge a weary nation into war again. They were aware of Britain's treaty obligations to Poland and the obvious threat of Nazi Germany, but many hoped against hope that there might somehow be a solution short of all-out war. After all, World War I, the worst bloodbath in human history, was still a fresh, evil memory; nobody wanted a repetition of that horror.

But men of vision saw that the coming terror was inevitable, and one of them—Conservative Member of Parliament Leo Amery—cut short the passionate debate: "Speak for England!" he said in answer to Arthur Greenwood, a Labor Party MP who sided with the wavering Chamberlain government, and by implication with appeasement of Hitler.

Winston Churchill, the tough, magnetic leader of Britain during World War II, was also the voice of the British people at their best. In the worst of times, he was the lion of the realm, roaring defiance of the enemy. Again and again, he spoke for his people and for the people of the Commonwealth, simply and to the point. He was never more clearly the spirit of Britain when he said to his country: "Nevah, nevah, nevah give in!"

The British didn't. They beat back the Luftwaffe during the perilous summer of 1940 with the strong and growing support of the Commonwealth, which bred some very tough sons of its own. This is the tale of one of them, and how he gave the Germans fits, enough fits for ten men.

When war broke out, Australian Charles Granquist was only seventeen, the son of a WWI veteran badly shot up in 1917. Charles grew up on his dad's hardscrabble farm, living in a tent for his first four years. He grew up working young, as most kids did in those Depression days, but he also did well in school. And when most of the world fell into war in 1939, he enlisted. The mother country was fighting, as Churchill put it, with her back to the wall, and the Commonwealth nations did not hesitate to go to her aid.

Young Granquist was no exception: He lied about his age and enlisted as an infantryman early in the conflict. His war began in January of 1940, with a troopship ride to Suez, where his battalion's passage to land gave rise to an incident that well characterizes the frontier spirit of the Aussies, and indeed all the British forces, for the captain in command was a proper, pukka Englishman. As Granquist told it later:

> *The captain:* "The sergeant will tell you where to go and what to do."
> *A voice from the ranks*: "Fuck the sergeant."
> *The captain*: "You hold him and I'll fuck him."

After some time in Egypt and Palestine, including the Sinai and Jerusalem, the battalion joined the successful British offensive in the Western Desert; Granquist's battalion was first into vital Tobruk. The going was good: An Australian brigadier who had captured a Turkish general in World War I took the surrender of an Italian admiral, some 1,500 of his men, and an Italian battleship, not an ordinary thing in the life of the infantry.

The battalion had covered itself with glory, but then came Greece, and the Germans, and the collapse of the Greek army. Granquist was wounded during the British retreat to the sea and was captured in May 1941 before he could find a spot on one of the ships braving constant air attack to evacuate the British and Commonwealth troops.

For some men, this would have been end of the road. As the Germans were fond of putting it to their prisoners, "The war is over for you." For Granquist and many of his comrades, however, it was just getting started.

He and other Commonwealth prisoners ended up in a camp at Wolfsberg, Austria, after a long trip on short or no rations. It speaks volumes for their spirit that even though they were deep inside Axis territory and they knew the war was going badly for the Allies, their thoughts turned almost immediately to escape. It was a tall order.

The living at Wolfsberg was graceless and the rations ranged from poor to inedible, but at that the British were a great deal better off than the Russian POWs in a nearby camp. Those men were on the edge of starvation, so hungry that, as Granquist watched, the Russians marched to collect rations by threes, two prisoners supporting a third man, quite dead, with an eye to collecting the corpse's rations as well as their own. The Russians paid dearly for their government's refusal to sign on to the Geneva Conventions on the treatment of prisoners of war.

By the early spring of 1942, Granquist and another man had planned an escape. They chose a day without work details, when the rest of the prisoners could help out. The two escapers had found and forced a window in a little-used room and went through it unobserved while the other POWs sang lustily to cover any noise they made. They chose a popular Gracie Fields tune, one that fit the occasion exactly: *Wish Me Luck as You Wave Me Good-bye.*

> Wish me luck as you wave me good-bye,
> Cheerio, here I go, on my way
> Give me a smile I can keep for a while,
> In my heart while I'm away.

Nobody among the Germans waved, and Granquist and his pal cut the wire—with a pair of stolen pliers—and got away clean. They headed south for Italy, moving at night and hiding out during the day. They traveled in uniform, since there was some likelihood that a prisoner found by the Gestapo might be murdered as a spy, as the Gestapo did later to many escapers. A few days out, Granquist had his twentieth birthday.

It was cold, as early April in the Alps is likely to be, and he and his companion had trouble resting at night, but the pair were young and tough and found Alpine Austria very much to their liking in spite of the chill; the population centers were concentrated largely along the floors of the valleys, and there was plenty of thick cover along the high ground above them. They made good progress, and in a week were close to the Italian border and the pass at Plocken, looking down at Italy. Here Granquist noticed something different and ominous: the good hillside cover of Austria was no more; on this side of the Alps, the terrain was, in his words, "bare as a badger's bum."

And that was their undoing. They made too much noise trying to avoid an Italian army frontier post, slipping and sliding on the ice, when "about half the Italian army came pouring out" of the post and it was back to jail. A month or so later, they were back in Wolfsberg, facing the usual punishment of twenty-eight days' solitary confinement on bread and water. Bread and water was exactly what their diet was, three days of it interrupted by a day of "regular" diet—bread, soup, and ersatz coffee. The soup was usually made of mangelwurzel, a sort of root vegetable generally used for stock feed. The brew was not popular.

The failure of his first try for freedom only whetted Granquist's appetite for another try, and now there was a new sense of urgency. He learned that all noncommissioned officers—he was by then a corporal—were to be transferred to a camp in Poland, there to vegetate for however long the war lasted. They would have the "privilege" of not working, but Poland was a lot farther away from anyplace an escaper wanted to go. What to do?

Why, become somebody else, that's what. And so he reached an arrangement with another prisoner, a man named Harvey who was enthusiastic at the thought of a move to a no-work camp. When the time came to move to a satellite camp, Granquist went as "Harvey," and before long he was gone through the wire again, headed for the Dalmatian coast of Yugoslavia with an Australian he called "Bill." Bill turned out to be a liability, for he insisted on sleeping in civilian shelter huts along the track—very dangerous places—and the two soon parted company.

Granquist almost made the Yugoslavian border but again blundered into a German patrol and ended up in an "absolute bitch of a place" called Markt Pongau, home to a batch of vile-tempered guards and about half the bedbugs and fleas on earth. Then it was back to Wolfsberg and another four weeks of bread and water. And more planning.

Granquist managed to convey news of his new name back to his family. He had been moved to still another camp for work in a quarry, a very tough place indeed; one exasperated New Zealand prisoner was shot and badly wounded after he told a guard to "get fucked," admittedly discourteous and incautious behavior, but in most places reason for no more than some time on bread and water or maybe a casual clout with a rifle butt.

Back to work. This time it would be a tunnel, which began under the bed of Granquist's next escape companion, Joe Wishart. This effort, timbered with bed slats, was driven toward the brush outside with the help of many prisoners, and the spoil was hidden in the ceiling. One guard—obviously not the smartest hen in the coop—found some of it but decided somebody was trying to grow mushrooms.

Granquist and Wishart got away clean and set out to the south. This time it was Plan B: trek all the way through Hungary, Bulgaria, and Macedonia to sanctuary in neutral Turkey. Within just a few days Wishart's health broke down and he could go no further. "I'm holding you up," he told Granquist, "I'll give myself up," and Granquist was on his own again.

He made good progress for the next four or five days and managed to get partway around Vienna until, as he put it, "I came round a corner and into the arms of two policemen." Then it was back to the multitude of hungry bugs at Markt Pongau and thence to more solitary confinement and more bread and water. Then Granquist was sent off to a disciplinary camp in eastern Austria.

There, he and others got in more trouble over the creation of a dubious home brew that they called "fong" for reasons unspecified. It was concocted of pears, apples, and potato peels and would knock down an elephant. Now that was the sort of misconduct the Germans understood, so there was no serious disciplinary repercussion.

In any case, it was time to think again about escape. By this summer of 1943, the Allies were plainly in the ascendant, and there were all sorts of rumors about the Italians calling it quits; if they were to do so, Italy was obviously the place to be. The prisoners' plans now centered on the best way to get there.

Granquist was to make the break with three of his mates, including Wishart, another Australian named Wolfe, and Hec Virgona, who spoke fluent Italian, an obvious asset where the little group wanted to go. Wishart and Wolfe went off together, and Granquist paired off with Virgona. Granquist had to wait a couple of days for Virgona, but elected to break out alone and wait outside in an isolated shack, where he was supported with food and news by an English prisoner, Dolly Grey. Dolly could move through the night like a phantom . . . or like a poacher, which was exactly what Dolly had been back in King's Lynne.

At last Virgona got out, and the two met and headed for what must have seemed like the Promised Land. Or at least it did until they found some Italian soldiers and gave themselves up. It turned out they were a little early. They found the air buzzing with talk of capitulation, but fear of the Germans was still too strong in spite of offers of money—British sterling, of course— from Virgona, who told the Italians he knew Winston Churchill.

And so it was back to Wolfsberg in handcuffs, crossing into German territory only a day or so before Italy actually surrendered.

The winter of 1943–1944 was a bad one, but it was also a time for more planning. It was also the time when Granquist started running under his real name again. With Jack Wooster and Ray Tietjen, he began to think about the Yugoslav coast, or maybe simply joining a partisan group in Dalmatia, and in late June the three cut their way through the wire and headed south through Slovenia, pointed for Croatia, Dalmatia, and the sea.

This time they were free men for almost two weeks. And then, with only five days or so to go to reach the sea, their dwindling food supply led them to make a major mistake, a call at a large farmhouse where an elderly couple and a younger woman fed them royally. They did not notice the disappearance of the young woman until she reappeared with German soldiers and they were back, as they British put it, "in the bag."

So it would be Wolfsberg again, solitary again—the finale of 196 days of it over the years as a POW—and, of course, bread and water again. The last escape had been the fifth try, and for Granquist it would be the last. The war was winding down; that was obvious to everybody, and even Granquist elected to sit the rest of it out.

There was some pleasure to it now, for the air was full of Allied aircraft flying north out of Italy. The local railroad marshaling yard was pasted around the clock, the Americans by day and the RAF by night. The prisoners mobilized to fill in bomb craters did their part for the Allied war effort by working at a speed as nearly glacial as possible. But the end was in sight at last, and it came as a sort of anticlimax. Two days before the actual ceasefire, the POWs' erstwhile jailors simply opened the camp gates and departed. The British spearhead was only some ten miles away, and Granquist took a flyer and telephoned the town they were said to have reached.

Against all odds, he managed to reach a British voice, of all things an officer of the Coldstream Guards. "Stand fast," the officer told him, "we'll be there before the Russians," who were then advancing from the east. No Allied POW wanted anything to do with the Russians, whose foul reputation preceded them.

And so it was. For Granquist and his friends, it was the end of four long years of confinement. Best of all, it was a bright beginning of a new life—for Granquist was not only going home, he was returning with a Russian girl who had been a prisoner at a nearby camp. She would become his wife.

Some stories really do have fairy-tale endings.

Chapter Six

The Wizards of MI9

EVERY MILITARY MAN OR WOMAN WHO'S BEEN IN UNIFORM more than twenty minutes knows that a fighting force is only as good as its information. You must know all you possibly can about your enemy: where he is, how he is equipped and disposed, who his leaders are, the state of his morale, and a dozen other things.

Technical intelligence magic—airplanes and drones and radio intercepts and such—can tell you some of this, but much of your information necessarily comes from people, agents of all kinds, professional and amateur. A few are traitors who sell out their masters for all sorts of reasons; the vast majority are patriots hazarding life, limb, and even family for their country.

These people are terribly vulnerable. There is no such thing as safety, and if they are caught, their only prospects are dim: torture and death. They know there is little hope of rescue, and if they are local people they know the horrible reprisals their devotion might bring to their friends and neighbors and family. And yet for love of country they willingly go out into the darkness among these hideous perils.

All of the heroism, ingenuity, and sacrifice of the agents in the field in World War II, all of the killing and the dying, would have counted for little in winning the war had it not been for the central brain that planned the operations and provided the intelligence and the training and the gadgets. In Britain, it was formally known as the War Office Directorate of Military Intelligence, and it was an immensely capable organism with many heads.

British Intelligence had many branches during World War II. Besides the familiar Domestic and Foreign Intelligence sections—MI5 and MI6—there were at least fifteen other specialized divisions, variously known as branches, directorates, and one division, that of Naval Intelligence. All had more or less defined responsibilities; all cooperated when they could, with each other and with their allies, especially the Americans.

The division called MI9 was charged with "resistance aid," a suitably amorphous term. In fact, its responsibilities included prisoner-of-war liaison and assistance, not only lending help to both Allied escapers and evaders but also handling post-escape interviews and providing intelligence feedback. The men—and some women—they helped were broadly classified as either escaper or evader, depending on whether they had ever been in Axis captivity.

MI9 was headed by forty-five-year-old Major Norman Crockatt, twice wounded and much decorated in the First World War. Crockatt, the thorough professional, was also a striking, memorable figure, given to wearing highland soldier's trews at every opportunity. He had a clear vision of what the agency's mission should be, as he later summarized it:

a. Helping Allied prisoners escape, not only regaining their services but also causing the Axis to commit more resources to security duty;
b. Helping Allied prisoners return to friendly territory;
c. Collecting and distribution information;
d. Denying information to the enemy;
e. Maintaining British prisoner morale.

Besides MI9, a number of other allied agencies ran clandestine missions deep in German-occupied Europe. In addition to the American Office of Strategic Services (OSS) and Britain's Special Operations Executive (always called SOE), there were the regular military intelligence services and various other sources within the Foreign Office and elsewhere in the government.

In America, MIS-X was born, a sort of twin brother to MI9, with which it worked very closely, sometimes in combined teams. MIS-X kept in close touch with American POWs at more than sixty German camps and was instrumental in many of the more than seven hundred American escapes. The United States, like Great Britain, had her own growing pains in the increasingly complex world of military intelligence: From a prewar establishment of fewer than seventy, by 1944 the MIS-X staff had jumped to almost 1,600.

Its boss, W. Stull Holt, was a WWI veteran, a university academic who took to his new job like a duck to water. From the first, his cooperation with, and feeling for, MI9 were close and cordial. His relations with MI9 and its boss, Norman Crockatt, were also warm and friendly, and Holt's choices as subordinates were solid and lasting, among them Colonels Ed Johnson, heir to the Lucky Strike fortune, and Catesby ap C. Jones, descendant of Catesby ap R. Jones, who had commanded *Merrimac* when she fought it out with *Monitor* in 1862.

By the time MIS-X was up and running, MI9 was a going concern, and the Americans were quick and willing to learn. And much of the technique and procedure of the British apparatus was adopted by the Americans in part or entirely. As Catesby Jones put it, "The British have a functioning underground in France. It is efficient enough to chart the progress of all evaders. I believe it unlikely that we could set up as successful an organization."

Most of the preparation and thought about escape and prisoner liaison had been rudimentary or even notional at the start of the war, in part a reflection of the general belief among the general public that there would never be another bloodbath like the kaiser's war. But the handful who were attracted to this "war in the shadows" and knew it had to be planned for were a special lot.

For instance, Major J. F. C. Holland, later innovator of the Commandos, started out as head of a tiny "research" branch in the War Office in 1938. The entire office staff was precisely two: Holland was one and his secretary the other, and at first Holland had carte blanche to research about anything he wanted to.

But Holland, badly wounded in WWI, had worked with the innovative genius of irregular warfare, T. E. Lawrence—"Lawrence of Arabia." Holland also become a devotee of warfare outside the book and, like his mentor, would achieve marvelous things. He had, according to a friend, "an independent mind, and an acute brain . . . quick, imaginative, and of a fiery temper." He was the sort of man MI9 could use.

Nobody underestimated the risks involved in the business of widespread prisoner rescues. Still fresh in everybody's memory was the execution of British nurse Edith Cavell by the Germans in 1915 for helping some six hundred cut-off British troops escape to neutral Holland. The incident was an early example of Teutonic *Schrecklichkeit*, but only a pale sample of the horror to come.

Over the course of World War II, guards of the regular German forces were, by and large, reasonably humane; generally, they followed the rules of war and the provisions of the Geneva Conventions. Men in the regular military component understood that it was the right and duty of prisoners of war to try to escape, subject to limitations imposed on POWs by treaty.

But the SS and, especially, the Gestapo were their usual brutal selves, led on by the all-time hoodlum, Adolf Hitler. The Gestapo would have liked nothing better than to gain control of the POW camps, and they repeatedly tried to do so; to their great credit, the regular military branches staunchly resisted that disaster, but many escapers fell into Gestapo hands, with terrible results.

It's worth adding here that Hitler himself was only alive because of an act of mercy by a British soldier during WWI. The Englishman, an extraordinary man named Tandy, was a veteran sergeant, a heavily decorated man, but he was also compassionate. He had held his fire, letting the wounded, helpless Hitler live. Hitler knew he had been saved by an Englishman's act of mercy and even knew who had given him the gift of life, yet he still persisted in his brutality toward British prisoners.

At the beginning, MI9 operated out of a single room. Everything was in short supply, including personnel, and there was a measure of competition with other "cloak and dagger" organizations such as Special Operations Executive and something called the Political Warfare Executive. MI9, like so much of the intelligence apparatus, grew by fits and starts, but it found first-class personnel when it needed them, men like J. M. Langley, who lost an arm at Dunkirk as a junior officer in the elite Coldstream Guards. Taken prisoner, he managed to escape and get back to England in spite of his wound.

He was the sort of man MI9 wanted, the first leader and at first the entire staff of Room 900. Before he and his stablemate Airey Neave were through, they had managed the safe return of some three thousand Allied personnel. But following Crockatt's blueprint, the infant agency later took some more space in the Great Central Hotel, where evaders could be interviewed, and finally moved outside London to Wilton Park, an estate near Beaconsfield.

One of MI9's most important functions may be called the Gadget, Thingamabob, and Doo-dad Department, headed by a genius named Christopher Clayton Hutton, known to all and sundry as "Clutty." His boss described both his value and his temperament exactly in a letter written—significantly—to an Army provost marshal officer: "This officer is eccentric. He cannot be expected to comply with ordinary service discipline, but he is far too valuable for his services to be lost to this department."

Hutton was a single-minded man, who operated out of a bunker he had built in a field near Wilton Park, apparently for privacy. There he developed all manner of useful items, from the escape tools so useful to downed flyers to more lethal gear such as specialized grenades and a sort of blowgun.

His handy products included escape maps—printed on silk. It was more expensive, to be sure, but silk was easier to hide and safely used because silk didn't make rustling noises the way paper did. Then there were tiny compasses, carefully secreted inside buttons or pens.

To get at some of them you had to unscrew a little cap or cover. Clutty thoughtfully equipped these with left-hand threads, so that if a curious German thought he might have found a concealed recess, his attempts to open the top would only tighten the cap. Other little compasses, disguised as buttons, you could use simply by scraping away their paint with your fingernail. All in all, he oversaw production of well over two million of the little navigation aids.

Some footwear was built with cloth leggings that could be turned into a reasonably convincing semblance of a civilian shoe. There were hollow heels in which you could hide contraband, and replacement uniforms sent to prison camps often were designed for easy conversion to civilian clothing. He also fabricated a special escaper's knife, an all-purpose tool that neatly included everything from saws and a lock pick to a wire cutter.

Then there was the steel pencil clip that also doubled as a compass, balanced on the point of its own pencil on a tiny indentation in the clip. That made a fine companion piece to a tiny saw, punched with a hole at one end so you could hang it down your trouser leg or suspend it out of sight in about any narrow crevice. A skinny surgical saw could disappear as a bootlace.

Hutton had specialized help. Among other assistance, he used the ingenuity of a professional magician called Jasper Maskelyne, who developed all manner of ingenious hiding places: hollow cricket bats, real money stashed in Monopoly games, maps hidden in playing cards, and the like. There are all kinds of fantastic stories about Maskelyne, tales of wondrous feats of hiding whole masses of vehicles, people, and other things, tales that in some cases look very much as if they were vastly inflated. Nevertheless, some of his contributions to the shadow war remain real and valuable.

Hutton's achievements were demonstrably the real thing. There were even phonograph records designed to hold false documents. Hutton also invented the plastic "escape box," modeled after a fifty-cigarette packet, a sort of magic collection of whatever an escaper/evader might need, from fishing line and hook, halazone tablets, and needle and thread to razor and magnetized blade to a collapsible rubber water bottle. A welcome addition was some money and a map of whatever country you were flying over.

There is the story of a squadron of irrepressible Poles, who conned a bank teller into turning all its emergency money into British pounds . . . and throwing a colossal party with the proceeds. The disappearance of Her Majesty's money led to an inquiry from MI9, and a glib explanation from the Poles. As Crockatt loved to relate the tale, he was innocently told, "Well, sir, I thought you would like us to celebrate the fact that none of us had to use the money."

The shipping of escape aids to the prison camps posed special problems as well. Neither MI9 nor MIS-X would use Red Cross parcels; those were the product of a respected international charity, open-handed to all sides. The use of Red Cross channels to cover the shipment of contraband was not tolerated, even in the good cause of escape.

Shipments from other "charities" were a different matter. Entities with all manner of convincing names were created as covers by which to send good things to POWs. So were private shipments purporting to come from families. Since family parcels and those from respectable-sounding charities were automatically suspect, concealment of escape aids quickly became an art form.

And there was the perpetual need for up-to-date identification documents of many kinds, a perpetual preoccupation with the Germans in occupied Europe, as it is with totalitarian regimes generally. Some of these required photos. There were requirements for travel permits—those varied depending on whom you were pretending to be—plus work permits and other specialized documents.

The Allied document forgers also had to learn to duplicate German handwriting; anybody who has served in Germany knows that old fashioned "Gothic" script looks like something from an Egyptian pharaoh's tomb. To avoid too-close scrutiny by the enemy, any document had to look suitably weathered: The real documents were carried and used every day, so clean, crisp pages invited inspection and arrest.

Some escape aids were special requests, like the one from the Escape Committee in formidable Colditz Castle. They needed a detailed map of that ancient, complex place to aid their perpetual and surprisingly successful escape planning. Hutton found a way to provide one.

USAAF crews carried small "escape purses," packets containing little saws and maps, photos in civilian clothes, and some currency useful wherever they were bound. Another gimmick was a little "phrase card," which gave some helpful things to say to the locals—the thing was often called the "pointy-talky": simply point to what you wanted to say and presto! communication, assuming, of course, that the person you addressed could read.

The pointy-talky was something of an improvement on the old "blood chit" that had been carried by RAF pilots as long ago as the colonial campaigns of the early twentieth century and the Americans of the Flying Tigers serving China against the Japanese before America was officially at war. The blood chit promised rewards to anybody helping the airman, usually in several languages.

Besides the well-organized prison breaks talked about in other chapters, there were many memorable individual efforts, like the storybook escape of American pilot Captain Jack Ilfrey, who managed not just one escape but two. The first was an unauthorized departure from neutral Portugal, where Ilfrey had landed when his P-38 fighter malfunctioned during a ferry flight.

The story goes that Ilfrey was seated in the cockpit of his again-functional aircraft, pontificating to the Portuguese on its virtues, when he seized the opportunity to crank up the aircraft and fly away to safety. Shot down later over northern Europe, he covered over a hundred miles to safety by bicycle, successfully pretending to be a deaf-mute.

One spectacular escaper was Wing Commander Basil Embry—later Sir Basil and an RAF air marshal—who early in the war bailed out over France, escaped, was twice recaptured, and twice more escaped, leaving, as one history chastely put it, "the odd sentry dead behind him." Embry showed up at last in England stylishly clad in clothing he had purloined from a French scarecrow—top hat included. A rising star in the RAF, he was a vigorous and outspoken advocate of the importance of escape and evasion doctrine and training.

The first prize for ingenuity has to go to the Royal Navy, however, in the person of Lieutenant D. P. James, who decided to escape in his own uniform, reasoning that few people in inland Germany had ever seen a British naval officer. He equipped himself with a forged identification card, calling himself "I. Bagerov" of the Bulgarian Navy.

Walking away from a shower detail—his friends covered his absence with a dummy—James made it all he way to Luebeck in North Germany before he was caught. (A second attempt, this time disguised as a Swedish sailor, was successful.)

Airman naturally gravitated to the notion of escape by air, and at least once the idea actually succeeded, or at least it did according to Maskelyne. Ditching in a Sicilian lake and captured, the crew of a British aircraft was flown off to captivity in a Savoia bomber—at least, until the RAF men took over the Savoia and told the pilot to fly them to Malta; if he didn't, they said, they'd crash the whole plane and kill everybody. The crew believed them, and the Brits landed on friendly soil, one of them waving something white out the window to stave off British fighters.

There are several similar stories, more than one involving escapers who got aboard an Axis airplane, only to find it did not have a self-starter. In one incident, two British pilots got as far as a Luftwaffe aircraft that did have its own starter, only to be frustrated by engines reluctant to turn over in the ice-cold weather.

Not all of the agents of MI9 were men. The women were as courageous and effective as the men, and several of them deserve extra-special mention. The founder of the so-called Marie-Claire escape line was, as the lawyers say, *sui generis*, one of a kind. She was English, born Mary Lindell, a nurse in WWI and now of high social position as Comtesse de Milleville. A lady of impeccable connections, she was also a fearless woman of powerful will.

Madame le Comtesse exercised that will on General von Stuelpnagel, commanding in Paris, and charmed him out of a heap of gasoline coupons, plus permits for herself, a child, and a couple of helpers. These resources were supposed to help her move orphans in the south of France; instead, her passengers were British evaders. She finally got crossways with the Paris Gestapo, and after some time in jail got out to England by way of Barcelona. There she was recruited by MI9 and returned to France by light aircraft late in 1942 to resume operation of her escape apparatus.

Then there was Andree ("Dedee") de Jongh, only twenty-five, the moving spirit of the Comete Escape Line. With her father and Elvira de Greef, called "Tante [aunt] Go," she came to specialize in aircrew, on one occasion moving seven bomber crewmen from the Dutch-Belgian frontier to Gibraltar in just a week.

Another stalwart of MI9 was also a three-time escaper, a man who had blithely tried to walk out of Colditz Prison dressed as a German *Gefreiter*, a corporal. The dreadful dye job of his home-made German uniform not only prompted his recapture but also provoked gales of laughter from the Germans. His third try went better, and he was back in England, where he would be of immense help to other POWs. This was Airey Neave, after the war a Conservative Member of Parliament, later murdered by an IRA bomb.

Neave joined MI9 on his return to England, becoming half the original staff of what would be I.S.9(d), a tiny office to control contacts with escapers and evaders all across northwest Europe. It generally was called simply "Room 900."

If an escaper or evader out of the eastern prison camps could make it west across the French border, he stood a vastly enhanced chance of staying free, particularly in the latter days of the war, when the French Resistance was at its strongest.

There were three fairly well-defined escape routes originating in France, called the Shelburne, the Comet, and the Pat (or, somewhat mysteriously, the P.A.O. or O'Leary line). The Pat and the Comet ran far south into Spain, terminating at British Gibraltar. The Shelburne ran to the English Channel near a place called Plouha, in Brittany, where Royal Navy motor gunboats took long chances to successfully manage several hundred over-the-beach rescues.

Once in the hands of the Resistance, an escaper or evader would be passed down the line, moving from safe house to safe house, like still another American pilot. He spent two months traveling on the Shelburne line before he made the channel and a safe pickup by the Royal Navy on the coast; he came home safe to England.

There were heroes uncounted throughout the history of escape during Hitler's war, many of whom, sadly, will never be known. There were the military prisoners, of course, those who dared the risks of escape and the cellars of the Gestapo, and those who dug and watched and forged and stole to help them.

Then there were the British and American pilots who landed rescue aircraft as big as C-47s in farm fields behind the German lines in the bowels of the night; and there were all the ordinary civilians who helped along the way, those who died in foul prisons if they were detected, and those who simply disappeared.

Nobody can give enough credit to the unsung escape organizations and all the prisoners who worked in them without a prayer of escaping themselves. Besides the diggers and dirt-spreaders and scroungers and forgers, there were the "duty pilots." Working by roster in shifts of one or two men, they watched the entry to the prison compounds around the clock, carefully recording the entries and exits of the guard contingent. They could, in theory, say how many guards were on duty at any moment and, generally, where they were in the compound.

There is a story that a senior German NCO, angry at the sloth of his own men, asked to borrow the British duty-pilot log to find out who of his own people was present when he was supposed to be . . . and who was slacking. At Colditz, the prisoners jury-rigged a warning system out of stolen German Christmas tree lights.

Altogether, something more than 26,000 British and Commonwealth escapers and evaders returned to serve again against the Axis. These were dedicated, experienced men, many of whom were highly trained, such as the aircrews. Ninety percent of the evaders and about a third of the escapers got out due at least in part to MI9's work.

It was quite a record for an ad hoc outfit that began life in a single room.

CHAPTER SEVEN

The Man Who Wouldn't Quit

IT IS REMARKABLE ACHIEVEMENT FOR A MAN TO RISE TO THE rank of wing commander in the Royal Air Force; it is equally remarkable for a man to knock down (conservatively) twenty-two enemy aircraft. But for a man to do all of these things supported by two aluminum legs is nothing short of miraculous.

But that is precisely what Douglas Bader did, the only pilot on record to do such a thing. Bader had been a brilliant prewar acrobatic pilot, chosen to compete on the RAF team at the Henley meet, the Olympics of competitive flying. He was also a champion at rugby and cricket, a good-looking kid who fluttered a lot of hearts among the ladies.

But then came the 14th of December, 1931, when flying across a runway right on the deck—in a right-angle bank with his wings at the vertical—he caught a wingtip, and his little Game-cock biplane clobbered in. Providentially, his harness kept him in the cockpit and the airplane did not burn, but when frantic ground personnel pulled him from what little was left of the airplane, he was nearly dead; the ambulance dashed to the hospital with an attendant holding one of Bader's femoral arteries closed with his fingers. Among other things, his legs were so badly damaged that they both required amputation.

In the ordinary course of things, for the ordinary man, that would have been the end of Bader's flying career, for although the Central Flying School passed him as capable to fly, the best government bureaucracy would do was a job on the ground. For a man with Bader's temperament, that simply was not good enough. His courage and determination would not admit of defeat in a profession so important in his life.

Happily married and playing professional-level golf in his spare time, he left the RAF for a while and worked for an oil company, but his heart remained, as Lord Tennyson put it, "in the central blue." And with the outbreak of war, Bader asked to return to active duty. This time, with every pilot needed to turn back the German attacks on Britain, he was returned to flight status and soon rose to command a squadron of fighters. Although his concentration was on teaching and leading his young pilots, he still had twenty-two confirmed victories, probably more.

He rose to wing commander, leading three fighter squadrons in the fighter sweeps over the Continent that followed victory over the Luftwaffe in the 1940 battles of England. The sweeps were aggressive sorties, gaggles of fighters out looking for trouble, taking the war to the enemy's own ground.

And then in August 1941, Bader went down over Le Touquet. Bader said later he thought that another aircraft had rammed him; legendary German fighter ace Adolf Galland thought one of his men had brought Bader down. Later research concludes it is more likely that Bader's fighter was downed by "friendly fire" in the wild confusion of the dogfight. He parachuted to safety.

And so Bader passed into captivity, again legless, since his artificial limbs had been badly damaged during his parachute landing. The Luftwaffe was sympathetic and patched up his damaged legs as best it could, but repairs left something still to be desired.

He soon set about the business of escape.

His first try came when he was still in the hospital at St. Omer. He broke out by climbing down from a window on a rope of sheets knotted together, fifteen of them, most contributed by other British patients. He descended into stygian gloom, uncertain how far from the ground he was, or whether the rope of sheets would reach that far. He had some trouble boosting his legs through the ward window, but once out his powerful arms and shoulders got him quickly down and to the welcome discovery that the sheets did in fact reach the bottom.

He went into hiding with the help of sympathetic French citizens. A local farmer gave him shelter, but he was betrayed by a collaborator.

Galland and other German pilots entertained Bader, "lavishly," as one account put it. He was allowed to sit in the cockpit of Galland's ME-109, and there was much conversation about the relative merits of the 109 and the Spitfire. During a conversation with Galland, Bader had the temerity to ask whether he could take the aircraft up, for "just one circle over the airfield."

"I nearly weakened," wrote Galland later.

Galland arranged for a drop of a set of replacement legs by the RAF, flying in to drop at a particular spot under a safe conduct. Bader told Galland just what should be passed to his wife, precisely where his spare legs were parked in their home. Also on Bader's list was a decent uniform and a new pipe, replacing the one that had been broken in the crash and was now patched together with tape.

And delivery was made, by the RAF, but not quite as scheduled; they also dropped some bombs about the same time, which some of the Germans, including Galland, felt was a little unsporting, but Bader had his legs.

Air Marshal Sholto Douglas later got a telephone call from Winston Churchill, saying rather grumpily that

"I see from the newspapers you've been fraternizing with the enemy, dropping a leg to a captured pilot."

Douglas had his answer ready: "Well sir, you may call it fraternizing, but we managed to shoot down eleven of the enemy for the loss of six or seven of our own, so I hope you might feel it was worth it."

It was good enough for the prime minister and, given Churchill's own spit-in-your-eye propensity for derring-do, probably warmed his heart.

Again relatively mobile, and with the respect of both his fellow prisoners and his captors, Bader might have lived out the war in the comparative comfort and safety of a Luftwaffe prison camp. But that sort of thing was not in Bader's personality, as enterprising and aggressive as it's always been.

In the first place, the Germans insisted on depriving him of his legs after his first escape attempt, at first even carrying him to the latrine. That indignity infuriated him and may well account for his loathing for his captors, a detestation that continued throughout his captivity, lending weight to his statement that "I am not one of those who regard war as a game of cricket."

Bader's temper did not improve when he was first lodged in a civilian jail. He caused such a ruckus that he was moved to a Luftwaffe transient jail. He continued to be a monumental pain, absolutely refusing to cooperate, including testifying for the defense at a court-martial of the staff at the hospital from which he had escaped. He also became part of an escape party driving a tunnel under the wire. Because he wasn't much use for digging, he played "stooge," lookout for interfering guard personnel.

Before the tunnel was complete (it was later discovered), Bader was moved to Brussels to testify in the court-martial of the hospital personnel from whom he had escaped at St. Omer.

In the end, he was transferred to Oflag VIB, a dismal camp near Luebeck, full of other officers half-starved on insufficient rations—those that the guard detachment did not steal. It came as a great relief when the camp closed down and everybody was moved by cattle car to a new, large camp at Warburg. Along the way, other enterprising prisoners cut a hole in the car's floor and one by one escaped through it . . . until one officer misjudged the drop and was killed by the car's wheels.

At Warburg, Bader's favorite occupation was goon-baiting, the gentle art of irritating the more obnoxious guards just short of getting beaten or shot; Bader was a past master at the game. He also joined in still another escape attempt.

Just outside the wire was a shed used for clothing issue. Bader and three others managed to go together to the shed; then, while other prisoners created a diversion, one of them picked the lock and they slipped into an unused room. Then, after full dark, after another diversion to lure away the spotlights, they left the shed and walked down a lighted path past some German huts to freedom. The camp's Escape Committee had equipped them with Reichsmarks, forged passes, maps, a compass, and homemade rations.

Their plan, however, was frustrated by something well beyond their power to plan for: a guard's bladder. When the goon emerged to fix his pressing problem, he almost walked into the four prisoners and yelled for help.

A second tunnel was partially successful. As usual, Bader was enthusiastic; while he could not hope to make it around a right-angle bend in the tunnel, he could certainly crawl that far, and another prisoner volunteered to follow with his legs. That plan misfired when it was discovered that the tunnel emerged— beyond the wire, all right—but in the middle of the path walked by two sentries.

Five men made it out, timing their run from the exit hole for the moment when both sentries were walking away from the hole. Sadly, it was a moment never again repeated, and with daylight the tunnel was discovered.

Next in Bader's odyssey was a move to Stalag Luft III, at Sagan, between Breslau and Berlin. The business of escape planning never missed a beat, this time with the added complexity of yellow sand lying beneath the drab surface earth; the sand was immensely tough to hide, the same difficulty that would later be encountered in the Adventure of the Wooden Horse.

While others dug, Bader fumed. He could not help with the work, especially under the very difficult conditions at Sagan, but he elevated goon-baiting to a fine art. Finally the Germans had enough and told him he was to be moved. Predictably, he refused; in the end, no fewer than fifty-seven guards—with their helmets, rifles, bayonets, and all—appeared to escort Bader from the compound.

Bader would not push it further; a confrontation might end in prisoners being killed or injured. And so he went along peacefully, even strolling through the ranks of guards as if he were inspecting them, to the intense amusement of the other prisoners. So it was that an oversize platoon of armed men managed to move a single, unarmed officer with tin legs. And as a finale, when the German guard wheeled to escort Bader to transport, fifty-six of them turned one way and one the opposite way, to roars of prisoner laughter. It had been quite a show.

Bader was now moved to Stalag VIIIB, a camp of some twenty thousand prisoners, and again his first thought was escape. The Escape Committee was sympathetic. Bader and a flight lieutenant named Palmer were slated to go on a working party with an Australian and an English NCO; a fifth man would be a Palestinian, a Polish Jew who spoke fluent Polish. They were destined for Poland, and Bader and Palmer got the usual documentation from the Escape Committee.

They joined the work party carrying their (smuggled) brooms, and while everybody milled around by the gate, two real working-party members busily swept their way back through the gate while Palmer and Bader swept their way forward to be counted through with the rest of the work party.

The walk to the work site was agony for Bader. The other prisoners helped him as much as they could, but they could not risk everybody's safety for that of one man. That problem was solved by delegating to Bader the humble role of latrine cleaner, who was allowed to remain in the latrine through the night. Outside there was only a single strand of wire, and beyond that, cornfield.

But his try for freedom didn't get that far. Before nightfall, the Germans called a formation, and when the order was given that all prisoners would drop their pants, Bader knew who had been found missing. He stepped up. "I'm the man you're looking for," he said.

Palmer was also captured, but the other three men got away. Two were recaptured and shot by the Germans, but the Australian NCO succeeded in joining the Polish partisans, fought with them for two years—including the bloody Warsaw rising—and then won his way back to England.

For Bader, the incorrigible escaper, it would be the end of the line, Colditz Castle, home to a select collection of officers who had to be perpetually watched and monitored. They were the incorrigibles, the perpetual escapers, and Bader was in select company. There had been very few escapes at Colditz; tunneling through the solid stone of the castle was virtually impossible and so was going over the walls, but everybody dreamed about a break.

But first Bader had to deal with a cockamamie charge of espionage. His response was logical: I'm in your prison, how can I possibly do anything that would amount to espionage? That, he was told, would have be decided by a court in Berlin. His apprehension ceased when word came that the charge had been determined to be frivolous. Bader survived another year of confinement, probably his hardest. It was the last year of the war, Red Cross parcels no long arrived, and emaciation had shrunk the stumps of Bader's legs so that walking was both chore and agony. The last days were also dangerous, as shells exploded on the castle, announcing the approach of the Americans.

Bader hitched a ride back west with an American pilot and was warmly welcomed by a set of American officers. Their commander called to him: "Come on, Doug. I've got your wife on the phone."

Douglas Bader was going home.

Bader never forgot about other people who had lost limbs and spent much time helping them. A foundation in his name continued to help the limbless long after Bader was gone. And Britain never forgot Bader, the sort of pocket lion so dear to the hearts of the British people. In the autumn of 1945, he flew a Spitfire in the Battle of Britain commemoration flyover.

He died of a heart attack in the autumn of 1982. Active to the end, he was on his way home from giving an after-dinner speech at London's Guildhall. He was honored with a memorial service at beautiful little St. Clement Danes on the busy Strand in London.

It had been quite a life. Nobody who met him would forget him, especially the Germans who had tried so hard to keep him in prison.

CHAPTER EIGHT

Deliverance from Evil

NOBODY LIKED BEING A PRISONER OF WAR, NO MATTER WHOM their captors were, but some of the enemy of World War II were better than others; the German regular armed forces as jailors were infinitely preferable to, say, the Gestapo. The Italians could sometimes be downright benevolent.

But down on the very bottom of everybody's list of favorites were the Japanese; their philosophy of Bushido, "the way of the warrior," and its accompanying contempt for a surrendered enemy made Japanese prison camps hell on earth. The POW's lot was not eased by the fact that Japan had signed, but never ratified, the Geneva Conventions on treatment of prisoners of war.

Nor were the Japanese given to using the first team as prison guards. Many of those in charge of POWs' daily lives were not Japanese at all—many were Korean—or were Japanese deemed unfit for service at the front. Many of these guards were given to taking out their—to them—shameful secondary military status by abusing the helpless, whether they were military personnel or civilians. In any case, the ordinary Japanese soldier was accustomed to being kicked around by his superiors; now he could do some kicking of his own.

All of which was a reflection of a national mentality, reflected by many prisoners' observations of gratuitous Japanese cruelty, such as bayoneting or decapitating prisoners, apparently just for amusement or practice. The Japanese attitude was pretty well summed up by a newspaper editorial comment about Americans:

> *They cannot be treated as ordinary prisoners of war . . . an eye for an eye. . . . Japanese Forces are crusaders in a holy war. Hesitation is uncalled-for, and the wrongdoers must be wiped out.*
>
> *Not that prisoners of any other nation were treated any better, nor were civilians, like the Filipino couple who were burned alive for aiding prisoners during the Death March . . . by providing a little food and water.*

Toward the end of World War II, there was also the matter of the Japanese shipping out thousands of Western prisoners so far held in the lands conquered by the Japanese, back when the going was good in the early days of the war. Later on, as the tide turned in favor of the West, any Western prisoners were herded into the filthy holds of down-at-the-heels freighters for shipment to Japan, Manchuria, Formosa, and other parts of the Philippines as slave labor.

Conditions and food on such ships were unspeakably bad as a norm, and a number of the ships—not marked as carrying prisoners as they should have been—were unknowingly sunk by American and British aircraft and submarines. Many thousands of prisoners died, a number conservatively estimated at twenty thousand, on what came to be called the "hellships."

In the Philippines, there was concern that the prisoners collected at Cabanatuan POW camp might suffer the same fate or simply be executed out of hand by the Japanese. In fact, the

Japanese command had already ordered the mass murder of camp inmates after the 1944 American landings in the Philippines.

One suggested method of disposing of prisoners was to herd a lot of them together, douse them with gasoline, and burn them alive. Maybe the idea was grounded in simple cruelty—there was certainly plenty of that—or maybe it was simply recommended to save ammunition. At least one such massacre had already taken place at a camp called Puerto Princesa, and the American command quickly planned a series of rescues; they knew they would have to move fast.

The Death March and subsequent maltreatment, murder, and illness had taken the lives of at least twenty thousand Allied prisoners, many more had died of illness or been murdered by their captors, and thousands more had already been shipped out, to either slavery for Japan's faltering war machine or a miserable death at sea.

By January of 1945, there were some five hundred prisoners left at Cabanatuan camp, many of them survivors of the Bataan Death March, almost all of them confined since the fall of the islands. They were mostly Americans, both military and civilian, with a handful of British, Dutch, and Norwegian prisoners.

At least 1,600 prisoners had been moved from the camp during the previous autumn, leaving mostly the sick and disabled. In fact, the camp was designated a holding area for sick prisoners, and one part of it—called the "Zero Ward"—was an area set aside as a place in which very ill prisoners could conveniently be sent to die.

The prisoners lived mostly on rice, supplemented by such meat as they could catch, including snakes and mice, and what they could grow on little plots inside the wire. They had some contact with the outside, however. Some was through their own jerry-built radios, mostly put together with purloined Japanese parts, but the best contact was the very active Philippine guerrilla organization, which not only served as a conduit for information—both ways—but helped the prisoners when it could. Among other things, the underground smuggled in thousands of tablets of quinine, the prisoners' only defense against the area's endemic malaria. The little pills saved a lot of lives.

Escape was always an option, and a number of men tried. The Japanese answer was a new rule: For every man who tried to escape, the camp guards would execute ten prisoners. At least one such execution was held, and twenty Americans were killed as a result. There were still plenty of men willing to chance death for their own freedom, but most men were unwilling to cause the murders of their fellow prisoners to save themselves.

Then, in January 1945, the camp guards abruptly moved out, leaving ominous warnings that if the prisoners tried to escape, the guards would know and would return to kill them all. Nobody knew whether the guards might still be lurking right around the corner. In any case, bodies of retreating Japanese troops regularly stayed at the camp, and other large Japanese forces were still stationed nearby, just across the Cabu River. With no helpful alternative, the prisoners stayed put, and by mid-January a large Japanese force had returned to reoccupy the guards' quarters. The prisoners guessed their arrival might well mean death for the surviving POWs.

The prisoners were helpless; any meaningful escape attempt had to come from outside and come quickly. When American troops went ashore in the Philippines and the Japanese command decreed mass murder of the prisoners, the American staff began immediately to plan. It was a straightforward Yankee solution. Go to the camps, kick the doo-doo out of anybody who gets in the way, get the prisoners out, bring 'em home.

The assets were there. In addition to a large, active Philippine underground, there was a very tough bunch of American Rangers (namely the Sixth Ranger Battalion), an equally tough reconnaissance unit called the Alamo Scouts, and virtually unlimited support from the navy and air force. The trick was to spring the raid suddenly and with total violence, giving no time for the Japanese to recover and use their gasoline or bayonets.

The camp at Cabanatuan was built as a rectangle, roughly 600 yards by 800, enclosed by no fewer than three eight-foot barbed-wire fences backed up by four-story guard towers and fighting bunkers. It was obvious that speed in penetrating the camp was of the essence. No raiding force could afford to give what Japanese were there, or nearby, time to even begin killing inside the wire.

The raid on Cabanatuan would be led by Lieutenant Colonel Henry Mucci, commanding the Ranger Battalion, on plans made by Lieutenant General Walter Krueger's Sixth Army Headquarters. War is the province of chance, and the best military plans can go badly wrong; this one had the great virtue of simplicity. Mucci would lead 120 Rangers; it was a small force, but since they had to march some thirty miles behind the Japanese lines to reach their objective, the trade-off between the security of fewer numbers and greater firepower seemed worth it.

Out in front of the Rangers by twenty-four hours would be two seven-man teams of Alamo Scouts, who would have up-to-the-minute intelligence for Mucci when he and his men arrived. The Scouts are well worth a word.

General Krueger had never forgotten the farcical American invasion of Kiska Island in the Aleutians, where much time and military energy was expended on invading an island the Japanese had already vacated. Krueger was determined that his men would have their own reliable, elite reconnaissance force, responsible to nobody but the Sixth Army. This elite little group was called the Alamo Scouts.

The creation of the Scouts had a double purpose. The first was obvious, long-range reconnaissance, and for that the Alamo Scouts had been well trained. The second purpose was not obvious to any casual observer: nothing less than killing General Krueger—on his orders—if ever he were in danger of capture by the Japanese. The general was privy to too much knowledge, for in addition to those things he knew as an army commander, he was one of the few privy to the secret of Ultra, the code-breaking operation that saved so many Allied lives in World War II. Any time the general was near the front lines, a detachment of Scouts was close to him.

The Scouts were hand-picked and chosen by the Sixth Army. Less than half of the applicants could complete the grueling six-week selection course, but the survivors were very valuable assets. Trained in all sorts of useful skills—from speaking rudimentary Tagalog to deciding which beetles were edible—they carried knives, the close-range weapon of choice, and also their choice of carbine, rifle, or submachine gun. That included the medical personnel, since the Japanese never had been respecters of the Red Cross.

The proof of the pudding was the Scouts' box score so far: Among them, 138 Scouts carried out a total of 106 missions. Besides the more than sixty Japanese prisoners they brought back for questioning, they left some five hundred enemy dead behind them. Some of the Scouts had been wounded, but not a single man had been killed in action to date.

They were good folks to have on your side.

The Philippine guerrillas also sent a contingent along, some eighty men who helped guide the American column and smoothed its progress through the Philippine villages. Another guerrilla column joined the Mucci force close to the objective, and its commander advised him to delay his attack for a day.

There were just too many Japanese, he said, including a thousand or so within a few hundred yards, another seven thousand a few miles away, and a whole division falling back down a nearby road.

Mucci wisely elected to wait another day, at least until the retreating division had moved on, and pulled back to a village a couple of miles away. He left two Scouts in an abandoned shack only three hundred yards from the prison camp, and the two produced a detailed plan of the target, the garrison's strength and disposition, points of entry, communication lines, and the like. It was ready for Mucci the next day.

Mucci would start his attack at 7:30 in the evening, with thirty Rangers drenching the rear of the camp with covering fire while ninety more hit the front of the compound to break the prisoners out. About a mile and a half away, 150 guerrillas were standing by with oxcarts to move the sick and emaciated prisoners back to friendly lines. A village schoolhouse was fitted out to serve as an ad hoc dressing station.

The larger American force had a long stretch of open ground to cross—they would have to crawl a long way, and there was only an hour or so in which to do it, between sunset and moonrise. There would be some major distraction for the Japanese, however: an overflight by a USAAF twin-engined Black Widow fighter, a spectacular low-level aerobatic exhibition that more than held the attention of the Japanese. The pilots, flying nap-of-the-earth in the dark, even cut and restarted one engine repeatedly, producing loud backfires.

One guerrilla force would hold the bridge across the Cabu River, to hold up the Japanese forces on the other side, and a second guerrilla unit set up a block against help from the main road in the other direction. Each guerrilla force had a bazooka in case they met hostile armor—there was supposed to be some—plus a couple of dozen mines.

The Rangers had tried to warn the prisoners that help was on the way; the day before, they had gotten a couple of kids to throw rocks among the prisoner barracks bearing notes that warned "be ready to go out," but apparently the prisoners thought the notes were either a bad joke or a Japanese trick.

A lot of things could have gone wrong but they didn't, and the break miraculously went almost precisely as planned. The decoy airplane's pilots held the Japanese attention with what seemed to be suicidally low passes over the compound, while the guerrillas cut the Japanese telephone lines, effectively isolating the garrison. A torrent of fire destroyed the guard towers and bunker, and a Ranger sergeant used his .45 to blow off the padlock that secured the main gate.

At first some of the prisoners thought the Japanese were attacking them and tried to hide inside the buildings of the prison compound. Once they realized they were being freed there were tears of joy, handshakes, and hugs, but many prisoners were so emaciated or ill that they could not walk alone and had to be helped out of their prison.

The Japanese were either dead, scattered, or heavily engaged by Rangers and the Philippine guerrillas. The only effective hostile fire came from a Japanese mortar. The mortar shells wounded several Rangers and prisoners, and mortally wounded the raiders' doctor, but effective return fire shut the mortar down after just three rounds.

Rangers had to carry many of the weakest prisoners from the compound. They would be transferred to oxcarts as soon as possible. Now, carabao (water buffalo) cruising speed is something around two miles per hour, but it was the only way to safety for many of the weakest men. Before the trek to the American lines was through, something like a hundred carts had been added to the rescue fleet.

Meanwhile, the Japanese across the Cabu River had come under heavy fire from a guerrilla contingent led by Captain Pajota, who also laid and fired an explosive charge that blocked any passage across the bridge that carried the road to the camp. The bridge still stood after the smoke blew away, but the monstrous hole in it made passage of any sort of vehicle impossible.

Japanese infantry tried to cross the Cabu on foot to attack, but the guerrilla defense at the battered bridge threw them back. Two tanks concealed in the brush were hit by the guerilla bazooka man, who had only learned how to use the thing a short time before, and about 10 p.m. the Japanese attack petered out. All that remained was the trek back to the main American position. It was hard, but as one prisoner put it, "I made the Death March; I can make this one."

Another Ranger was mortally wounded on the return trip—ironically by friendly fire—but friendly fire was helping the withdrawal too, including welcome strafing by Mustang fighters and more P-161 Black Widows, one of which accounted for a Japanese tank and five trucks. The plodding oxcart rescue convoy pushed on, but there still remained one more obstacle.

Paradoxically, it was Filipino, communist Hukbalahap guerillas, who twice tried to insist that only Americans could pass their village; Pajota's men, not being Hukbalahap and therefore enemies, could not. Mucci solved that problem in typical Ranger fashion, simple and direct. "Yes they can, and they will," he said; "either that or I'll call in an artillery barrage that will reduce your village to junk."

That seemed plain enough, and the Huks, not knowing that Mucci's radio equipment was inoperable, found his manner and his argument most persuasive, and their objection was abruptly withdrawn. The great ox caravan, by now over a hundred carabaos nose-to-tail, carried on plodding their glacial way toward freedom.

And then at last the long journey was over and the prisoners were safe at last, all 522 of them, including thirty-three civilians. Most were American, but there were twenty-three British and ones and twos of several other nationalities. One of the British escapers deserves special mention, soldier Edwin Rose, who had gone to sleep in the latrine and missed the whole action, even though other prisoners vainly searched for him. Once he woke to find himself alone in an empty camp, he still took the time to shave and dress in his best uniform; and then he walked out alone until guerrillas found him and led him out to the American lines, safe, sound, . . . and free.

One of only two fatalities in the Ranger force was their healer, Doctor Jimmy Fisher. Hippocrates would have been proud: Fisher's last words are said to have been, "Good luck on the way out." The other was the Ranger hit by friendly fire, Corporal Roy Sweezy. One prisoner died of illness during the evacuation, and another was so weak that he died just as he was being carried out the camp's main gate. "It was really sad," one Ranger commented later. "He was only a hundred feet from the freedom he had not known for nearly three years." Two Scouts, two Raiders, and some twenty guerrillas were wounded or injured.

The Japanese were not only acutely embarrassed but also badly bloodied. Estimates of their casualties range from five hundred to a thousand dead. The casualty list included seventy-three guards, about 150 retreating Japanese who were stopping at the camp overnight, plus the troops killed trying to cross the Cabu River against the ferocious resistance of Captain Pajota's guerrillas.

The rescue produced a lot of happiness among the freed prisoners . . . and at least one reunion. One of the Ranger raiders at Cabanatuan joyfully recognized one of the prisoners as a man he knew well, a man reported killed in action some three years before: his father.

CHAPTER NINE

Dedee's Way

I could not accept that a race, because of its blond hair and blue eyes, that this type of people would consider itself to be superior to all others, that it would rule, and that all other races would be considered sub-human. Could one passively allow such a thing to happen? No, it is better to die fighting than to accept such horrors . . . even if some of us had to lose family, or friends. Such commitment goes hand-in-hand with great sacrifice, and those of us in the Comete Line had more than our share of personal misery.
—Countess Andree de Jongh, GM
(Code name Dedee)

THE FIRST BRITISH AIRMAN DEDEE HELPED WAS JACK NEWTON, whose bomber had crash-landed in German-occupied Belgium. Jack joined the RAF volunteer reserve in 1938 with dreams of becoming a pilot, but a crash in flight school left him with only one option. He became a turret gunner for a Wellington bomber crew when the war began.

Their first assignment was flying a plane called "G for George" out of RAF Benbrook, dropping propaganda leaflets in France and Belgium. But that didn't last.

Their target late on the evening of August 5, 1940, was the railroad yard at Aachen, Germany, some sixteen miles from the Belgian border. If all went well, they would hit the target, perhaps some nearby factories as well and be back for breakfast by nine the next morning.

This was their first bombing mission. Into Germany they flew, as Jack gripped the Browning .303 machine guns in the front turret—one of the most exposed places in the airplane. According to Newton, they dropped some 3,250 pounds of bombs at the Aachen railroad yards just before the starboard (right) engine erupted into flames and quit. "George" made a run for the North Sea, so crippled that she barely missed the spires at the ancient cathedral in Antwerp, looming two football fields away when they first saw it. Within seconds, Newton yelled out that he had spotted a darkened airfield to the left. Pilot Roy Brouard Langlois hesitated, then murmured "let's give it a go" and banked sharply to the left, straining the single engine still running, he had no room to maneuver; all he could do was try to land on the blacked out enemy runway.

They somehow glide over Messerschmidtt fighters and other German planes to a perfect landing in complete silence. That didn't last. They heard a volley of shots, and German soldiers who had been in air raid shelters moments before fired up their Mercedes and drove toward them in the darkness, just as Jack Newton lighted up the wrecked bomber with six flares as a diversion for their escape. He wounded himself in the eye, yet somehow kept up with the others running for the enemy airbase fences, loaded down with pounds of flight gear they didn't have time to take off.

This meant freedom for some crew members but captivity for others.

"We are not going to stand a chance of avoiding capture if we stay as we are. We must split into two threes." Langlois ordered,

"Me, Jack, and Tich [Copley] in one group, McLarnon, Burry, and Poreous in the other." He wished the others luck and disappeared with his trio. Newton, Copley, and Langlois spent the next three hours trying to put a few miles between themselves and the Germans. Their goal was to find help in a church or monastery, then make for the coast.

Dawn of August 6 found them in a wheat field, where stalks harvested in tall bundles gave them a perfect place to sleep in hiding. Or so they thought. "Hello, are you airman?" a young man asked in halting English as he stopped his bicycle late that afternoon. Fortunately, he was in the Resistance and promised to return by dark.

As the dusk settled on the quiet countryside, they heard the high, squeaky voice of their young benefactor: "Ello please: are you Englees airmen?" Within minutes he led them to a farmhouse not far from where they were hiding. The farmer, Alphonse de Voegt, explained that they were in a small town near Antwerp, Belgium. Coffee served in a farm hayloft soon revived their spirits, but they could see fear in the farmer's face. And no wonder.

An intensive search for them had already begun. Still, despite the risk, de Voegt brought them some of his own clothes, which were then becoming scarce. Jack Newton picked a long gray overcoat and beret. They remained undercover in their hayloft hideout, dining on potato soup and occasional chunks of meat that had first been served the same day that they noticed the farm cats had disappeared. There was little to do, other than look at photographs in area newspapers they couldn't read. As a precaution, they buried all their military gear right down to the pocket knives.

Within a few days they were moved to Antwerp, a half-hour train ride from the de Voegt farm, guided by the twenty-something daughter of a local banker. The trio tried to be as casual as possible during their first encounter with armed

German soldiers at a train station. Their next stop was a "luxurious looking three-story house of great character with huge wooden garage doors and a palatial oak door." Their host had everything to lose by helping them, as Newton recalled sixty-two years later. The owner, Paul Duquenne, was a prosperous banker with good taste in art and furnishings.

When Duquenne brought in a doctor to treat Newton's injured eye, the RAF airmen learned that back at the airfield where they crashed, the Germans had at first assumed they were dead in the smoldering remnants of the Wellington bomber but began a frantic search for them when they discovered otherwise. Roadblocks, scout planes sent aloft, and German patrols did little more than warn the Resistance to be cautious. Their next guide, the girlfriend of their first rescuer, moved them to the home of a Doctor de Bie, who distributed Red Cross packages day and night from his home in a suburb of nearby Liege.

Their companions at the de Bie safe house included Resistance fighter A. G. Pasteger, who once managed the very factory the crew was assigned to bomb as a secondary target. At yet another safe house, they listened to King George VI encouraging the Allied forces on British radio. Newton and his two fellow crewmen had no way of knowing it, but there was now a serious problem.

The very night Newton and the others began hiding at the de Voegt farm, three dead RAF airmen had been fished out of the River Meuse at Liege. And now, their RAF uniforms were being worn by German impersonators to ferret out Resistance fighters and find British airmen. The Newton trio were soon moved again, this time to Bois-le-Compte, about fifteen miles from Liege; while they slept on the second floor of a spacious home, their host, a Mr. Francois, entertained the local Fascist consul in his formal living room below.

On the afternoon of August 14, 1941, twenty-one-year-old Resistance leader Emile Witmeur arrived to question Newton and the others. They were now taken to separate houses and questioned for several days. Finally, Witmeur delivered the news in person, after some contacts with British intelligence:

We had some reason to think you might be Germans in RAF uniforms trying to infiltrate our Liege organization, so we had to be sure you were not. Now there is no doubt that you are from the bomber that landed on the airfield.

If your answers had been wrong . . . I would have taken you into the yard and shot each of you in the head. There would have been no second chance.

They were still not out of danger. While being guided to a bridge in Liege, they encountered Paul Doneux, another Resistance leader who stopped Witmeur. "What have you done?" Doneux asked "These three men are not English, they are German. They have taken the papers on the corpses of the three [dead RAF] airmen who have been taken out of the water." But after another check with London convinced Doneux that they were British, Newton was now allowed more freedom. While staying nearby in a safe house, he was given a single instruction: Stay away from the window. Eventually, he was moved to a white villa in Waterloo, the village of Napoleonic fame; two German soldiers quartered there by order of the occupation authorities kept a machine gun in their room at night.

Some three weeks later, Newton strolled into the villa garden and beyond into a field just a few steps away—right into the view of an armed German guard whom he had to knock to the ground before running for his life. His next stop after this, back in Brussels, was hardly what he expected: "He could see it was a pleasant tree-lined road with quite tasteful two- and-three story individually architectured private houses. Jack knew he was going to the home of a single lady owner who lived there alone, but he had no idea that she was a nun."

And a gun-toting nun at that; Antoinette Becquet was a pleasant woman of about forty with strong features and a proud upright figure who spent several days each week at a nunnery nearby. Soon, Newton met her brother, a monk from a nearby monastery. Newton never learned his name, but the monk packed two Colt .45 pistols beneath a huge cloak that he used for smuggling. The friar visited the house at least twice a week. And there were some interesting people in Sister Antoinette's circle, notably Hubert Casin, a talented pianist and pilot who helped a number of Allied airman travel the Comete Line to freedom.

About ten days after arriving, Jack moved to one last safe house in the Brussels area before he was to cross into France. This time, Casin led the way to a noisy bus for a one-hour ride to a massive three-story pile where he met two other evaders.

Larry Birk, an Australian pilot, had stayed free by disguising himself as a priest, complete with cloak, cassock, and hat. Harold Carroll took the place of another pilot who stayed behind due to illness, while their false papers identifying them as Frenchmen living south of Paris were prepared. Jack became a salesman named "Jacques Dumonceau."

The Newton trio was told that they would not be traveling due west toward Britain as they expected. Instead, their longer but far safer journey would take them across the Pyrenees, through Spain to Gibraltar.

By September 8, they were back in Brussels yet again. Three days later Newton met Andree de Jongh, code named "Dedee," meaning "little mother," the twenty-five-year-old woman who had created the Comete Escape Line. The trio was hardly impressed in those early days. "Our lives depend on a schoolgirl," Australian pilot Larry Birk wisecracked.

Soon, Gerard Wacquez, a highly skilled saboteur specializing in bridges, joined them. And Dedee taught them all the ropes, starting with a favorite Gestapo trick drawing out even the most careful evader. "Can you tell me the time?" the investigator would ask; more often than, the hapless evader would instinctively give himself away.

Their next journey required three train trips just to reach a densely forested border crossing between Belgium and France called Quievrain. Dedee had tested this crossing several months before. She had guided ten Belgians and an English woman across the Somme there, even though half of them had to swim the hundred-yard river crossing on a rubber float.

From there, Newton and the others walked on toward La Corbie, a town some nine miles east of Amiens, then the most northern border of German-occupied Europe. And from Amiens, Dedee guided them by train into the very heart of Nazi-occupied Paris.

Their next stop was supposed to be Bayonne, but their connecting train from Austerlitz in the Netherlands was delayed. And so they took in a propaganda film at a nearby theater and some nightlife on their way back to the station; Jack Newton told his biographer years later that while they walked along they saw a truck full of Germans followed by a sleek black car. He knew instinctively that someone was in danger.

In previous operations, Dedee had developed an unusual technique to deflect attention. Shortly after leaving the station, the evaders would begin peeling, eating, and sucking on oranges, which seemed to put off other travelers. Jack Newton developed another technique himself: When another passenger tried to strike up a conversation, he simply buried his head in a newspaper.

Some six hours later, the inspector who had examined their papers poked his head into their compartment: "Bayonne in ten minutes," he announced. They were in southern France, about ten minutes from the Spanish border and nearly fifty miles from the safety of the British consulate in San Sebastian, on the far side of the always-challenging Pyrenees mountain range. And although Spain was in theory a neutral country, in practice it was sympathetic to the Nazis. Refugees, particularly Allied escapees, were unwelcome. Spanish border guards often shot them when identified, no questions asked.

Those things concerned but did not stop Dedee. Earlier, in August, she had made this journey. Her guide, known as Thomas, doubted she had the stamina to cross the Pyrenees, but she outpaced him in the mountains early one morning. The next day, she stormed into the British consulate asking for money and plenty of it. Eventually, she pitched the idea to the consul himself. "He told Dedee that he . . . found it difficult to believe she was capable of such a mission. That such a young girl, in white ankle socks, had crossed the hostile Pyrenees and had set up an escape line through Belgium and France to rescue crashed airmen." Dedee told him she had already made the one-week journey with two Resistance fighters. She led a Briton and a Scot starting from the family home owned by her father, Emile Verhaeren (code-named "Paul"), in the Schaeerbeck district of Brussels. She now asked the Brits for 600 Belgian francs to do it again.

Since she described her escapees as "packages," the British consul nicknamed her "the Postman" and began vetting her through his contacts in London. There were, of course, some complications to consider. The Comete Line extended over a thousand miles with many vulnerable safe houses along the way. And there were the informants, often Resistance members who had been arrested. One of them had mentioned Dedee to the

Gestapo earlier in 1941, prompting a visit to her family home that no Belgian wanted.

Two Germans drew up outside her father's house "in a grey-colored Opel, the bigger one with a briefcase tucked under his left arm, and pressed the bell firmly a number of times." Paul was inside, but couldn't answer the door until he had concealed some blank identity cards and some money that had been spread out on his kitchen table.

The Gestapo didn't ask to be invited in; they invited themselves, stomped their way up the stairs to a front room where the man with the briefcase opened it and prepared to make notes. "Where is your daughter?" the other one snapped. During the brief lackluster interrogation that followed, Paul told them that Dedee had left months ago. He knew instinctively that a Resistance prisoner had been forced to inform on them.

Paul, then fifty-six, was a geography teacher who had began conducting Resistance meetings at his primary school in a working-class neighborhood when Belgium surrendered in late May 1940. After Dedee created the Comete Escape Line, he had begged his daughter to become part of it.

Comete logistics were somewhat complicated. By early 1941, at least ten British airmen were hiding in Brussels. They were safe for the time being, but keeping them in one place for too long was dangerous. And to keep Resistance spirits up, Comete had to show results. Once on board, Paul recruited several key Comete leaders. Among them was Andree Dumont (code-named Nadine), a message bearer about Dedee's age, and Henry Mitchelli, who became Paul's chief assistant.

But the idea had been Dedee's, springing in equal part from boredom, her quest for adventure, and her admiration for Edith

Cavell, the English nurse executed during World War I at Brussels for helping British, French, and Belgian soldiers evade or escape from the Germans. Now, in 1941, Dedee was helping Jack Newton.

Dedee had established a string of safe houses from Brussels to the foothills of the Pyrenees and beyond, into Spain. The key to her success was the over-the-top German chauvinism, which was no mean feat in that era, as Dedee had experienced in her dealings with the British consul in San Sebastian. German soldiers simply could not or would not conceive of a twenty-five-year-old woman organizing a thousand-mile escape line extending from Brussels to San Sebastian.

Dedee, Newton, and the others pulled into Bayonne at six that morning, quickly eyeing the half-dozen German soldiers on the platform. Bayonne had been a family-friendly Parisian vacation destination before the war, but most of the passengers that August were businessmen. Janine, the teenaged guide who led them out of the station, had the keys to a little known exit near the restrooms leading directly to the street. From there they walked to a nearby café for coffee before the most dangerous part of their journey.

Their destination now was the de Greef house in Anglet, a nearby suburb whose town hall now served as the local German army headquarters. Conveniently their Comete host, Fernand de Greef, worked as an interpreter for the Germans and helped his wife, Elvire (code-name Tante Go) buy and sell goods on the black market, a common Resistance occupation.

While waiting at the de Greef house to make the Pyrenees crossing, Dedee scouted their route and told the RAF men what to expect during the trip with their guide, Florentino. The crossing would be very difficult, with "craggy climbing conditions, narrow, steep paths, dense fog preventing climbers from seeing anything more than a few feet in front of them, and heavy rain, even snow that can suddenly come from nowhere."

In mid-August, before the Newton party arrived, the de Greefs had hosted eleven evaders who had crossed the Pyrenees only to be arrested by the Spanish. But this time, Dedee had arranged for British assistance as soon as the Newton evaders had crossed the mountains. The numbers of evaders was ever increasing as more and more British airmen were shot down. The British radio service BBC even began broadcasting prearranged code words to alert the Belgian underground.

And now, four days after their arrival, the Newton evaders prepared for a seventeen-mile night bike ride to Urrugne, a Basque village near the Spanish border where they would be outfitted for the night hike. Although it was early September, they slipped on overcoats for the journey. A few hours later, they were sipping homemade vegetable soup, listening to the BBC back home.

Their guide across the Pyrenees was Florentino Giocoechea, a smuggler and black marketer who had become a local legend, as Newton's biographer described, whose help the Resistance wanted almost as much as the Germans and Spanish wanted to put him in jail.

He had broad shoulders, muscular arms, and a wide smile. Florentino gripped the British airmen's hands in welcome as if their lives depended on him—as soon they would. He warned them of the dangers ahead, as Jack Newton recalled later. "He [Florentino] warns us that the descent to the Bidassoa River [in the Spanish foothills] is going to be the trickiest bit, especially after the rain. The four of us began to get a bit nervous."

But Florentino had a secret weapon. This was the second of twenty-four 8,000-foot mountain crossings he was to make during the next three years. The first few miles were an easy walk along trails that had been scattered with wild geraniums and mountain lilies only two months before. But now the days were wintry and the climb was increasingly tedious; Newton remembered six decades later how the trail narrowed uncomfortably, even though he had extensive experience hiking in the Scottish Highlands.

The climb continued another half-hour that day, until Florentino thinks that a brief stop will be safe. They passed 8,000 feet but soon heard the river. "It is not good news that we can hear it from here." Dedee said, telling them that the Bidassoa River at Irun, an ancient Roman town, would be very difficult, if not impossible, to cross that day. She didn't have to mention that this would mean another seventeen-hour trek back to where they started.

Their hosts welcomed them back to Urrugne, although disappointment and fear were in their faces. Three days later, Dedee and Florentino began the hike to an alternative crossing five miles away. This time, they faced an aging neglected bridge swinging 100 feet above rapids, guarded on the Spanish side by soldiers who often shot to kill without asking a single question. The Newton group had little choice but to cross shortly after midnight when the guards would most likely be asleep. They got past the guardhouse, entered an abandoned railroad tunnel, and separated when the group emerged.

Gerard, the Resistance fighter, was headed to London for a new assignment and Florentino returned to lead others across the Pyrenees. As the British airmen, accompanied by Dedee, walked into a town called Renteria, children were laughing and skipping along the street, the war seemingly a million miles away, instead of just across the border nearby. Still on their guard, they took precautions. Jack Newton remembered years later, as if he were back in Spain, that the three of them sat apart to avoid attention. Once they arrived, Dedee led them to a café nearby.

The RAF evaders slept that first night in an abandoned water tower. Despite insect bites, they slumbered in relative safety.

Dedee woke them early the next morning for the walk to the British consulate at San Sebastian. Later, after some time hiding in the British embassy chapel at Madrid, Birk, Carroll, and Newton were smuggled into Gibraltar on January 7, 1942, and returned to England one week later. Although the RAF didn't quite know what to do with him, Newton eventually landed at the British Foreign Office where he worked in Security and Intelligence. He died in January 2004, officially acknowledged as the first British airman to evade capture and return home from German-occupied Europe during World War II.

Although Dedee and her Resistance smugglers expanded the Comete Escape Line operations, they were eventually infiltrated by the Gestapo. Dedee herself was arrested and tortured by the Gestapo but eventually released. They simply couldn't believe that such a large escape operation had been organized by a woman—and a twenty-five-year-old woman at that. The Gestapo had now been watching Dedee and her father for many months. They raided the de Jongh home again in early February 1942; shortly after that, Paul fled to Paris with a one million Belgian franc price on his head. He was captured there in 1944 and executed March 28, 1944, with a smile on his face, "knowing he had served his daughter and her Comete Escape Line to the bitter end."

Dedee helped over four hundred Allied soldiers and airmen escape from Belgium through France to Spain and Gibraltar. She personally guided some 118 airmen through the Pyrenees to freedom. After the war, Dedee spent the rest of her life in African leper colonies. She died in October 2007. Her funeral was held in the family parish church, a place frequented by St. Alice of Schaeerbeck, an early thirteenth-century saint who selflessly served the lepers of her age.

The two women had much in common.

CHAPTER TEN

Night Crossing

ON THE WALL OF BOB SMITH'S STUDY IN THE HILLS OF THE Ozarks hangs a painting of the 42nd Highlanders, better known to military history as the Black Watch. The regiment, resplendent in kilts and feather bonnets, is starting its advance up a hill at the battle of the Alma River during the Crimean War. Their objective is a great mass of Russian infantry, which the Scots propose to drive off the hill. That they will shortly do, with much panache and great slaughter of the Russian enemy.

The Black Watch was, and still is, one of the most famous regiments in the British Army. Its First Battalion was part of the British Expeditionary Force (BEF) that went to France in the autumn of 1939 in a vain attempt to shore up the crumbling French forces. Its expertise and spirit were sky-high, even if some of its equipment left much to be desired—for instance, the so-called Boys' "anti-tank rifle" in .55 caliber was a joke, and much other gear was outmoded, in short supply, or both. At one point, the entire battalion had to make do with a total of five maps—Michelin road maps at that.

For all that, the battalion's personnel were first class. They were professionals, both officers and enlisted men. The adjutant of the First Battalion was a remarkable young captain called B. C. Bradford.

Like so many British officers of the time, Bradford came from a military family. His uncle, a battalion commander, had been killed in the early days of World War I, and a second uncle died in the next year. His father had won the Distinguished Service Order in the same war and his grandfather had been a soldier in India, rising to become a provincial governor. Dozens of other relatives had also served with distinction. Bradford came of good blood, a soldier to his bootheels, and he was about to prove it.

When the German blitzkrieg smashed across France in 1940, the First Battalion of the Black Watch fought well in a hopeless effort. The BEF bloodied the Germans' noses more than once, but it could not hold the German advance alone, and the much larger French army was crumbling badly. During one British attempt to evacuate wounded over a beach, panicked French soldiers tried to push past the wounded and had to be driven back by British soldiers using hand grenades and bayonets; one estimate put the toll of French dead at about fifty.

The Royal Navy and a gallant bunch of small-boat skippers lifted more than 230,000 British and French troops to safety at Dunkirk, and there were successful evacuations elsewhere, but Bradford's battalion could not reach an open beach or port in time. Among other things, one attempt to move clear of pending encirclement was vetoed by the fumbling French command.

Accordingly, much of the battalion passed into German captivity, headed southeast toward imprisonment; but warrior Scots tend to be a contrary breed, and a good many men of the battalion immediately turned their attention to escape. Nobody wanted to spend the war as a *Kriegsgefangener*, and even food and water were in short supply. At one point, Bradford went three days without a meal, and when he brought some precious water to some of his thirsty men, German guards knocked him down and poured the water on the ground.

But before anybody thought of how to get back to Britain, they first had to deal with the problem of shaking off the Germans. Bradford was herded into a column of other British prisoners and marched off toward imprisonment. He and a number of other daring souls would not remain prisoners for long and almost immediately began to watch for likely chances to escape.

Bradford and some others got their chance as the column passed a swampy wood. The place was a morass and crawling with mosquitos, but it was free of Germans, at the moment much the greater pest. If a man could step casually into the wood when no member of the German escort was looking, he at least had a start. Bradford was among those who got into the forest.

Some of the escapers were both skillful and lucky; they equipped themselves with bicycles, made their way into Spain, crossed into Portugal, and were back in England in six weeks. For the rest, including Bradford, the going was much harder, but at least Bradford spoke a little French. First for him was the matter of some sort of disguise, and that meant getting local help. Bradford tossed a pebble at a civilian walking past his woods. The man turned out to be a Polish miner who promised to help and duly returned wearing two suits, one of which he peeled off and gave to Bradford.

It was a curious affair of striped trousers (too short) and a collarless white shirt and black coat. But at least it was civilian clothing, and, as Bradford said later, with the addition of a beret and walking stick, "I thought I looked quite like a Belgian refugee schoolmaster."

Bradford's first instinct was to head west, across the channel, but that proved to be impossible. There were too many Germans, so the only feasible route left was south. That way lay safety across the Pyrenees, to either Spain or Portugal. It was a very long trek, but maybe, with luck, it was a chance to make it all the way to Britain and get back in the war.

The hazards of travel across occupied Europe were many and constant. Ideally, a successful escaper needed a good sense of geography, physical endurance, friends, and, as one escaper put it, a double ration of luck. Now Bradford was a fit young man, knew his way around France, and was already finding friends, French people who risked their own necks to give him a place a sleep and what food they could spare, and the Polish miner who gave him his first disguise. There would be many more willing helpers.

He could manage only what he called "poor" French, but there were many foreigners in France at that time whose mastery of French was no better; some spoke it hardly at all, including the average German. To most *Boche* he was just a Frenchman speaking garbled prose, or "some kind of foreigner."

He started using his luck early on.

He was picked up by a suspicious German patrol, but satisfactorily answered questions in French and finally was allowed to move on. Then there was the German officer who halted his staff car and called Bradford to him. Bradford was braced for anything, but all the German wanted was directions to a French town. Bradford gave them and walked on.

Some of the French were afraid to shelter or feed him, some told him to go away, but nobody gave him up to the Germans. One man who might have done so was frustrated when his wife told Bradford what her husband intended. Some helped out enthusiastically, others were reluctant but still gave what aid they could. One helped out with a boat ride across a swollen river; another provided maps.

An aristocratic couple followed up this kindness with a gift of fresh clothing, money, more maps, and the luxury of private transportation, a bicycle. These same people, the de Bernards, were a continuing help to Allied military personnel on the run until their luck later ran out and they were imprisoned. They survived the war, but their health was irretrievable damaged. Their children's nanny carried on helping the Allies.

And then, on July 10, Bradford was caught, this time by the Vichy French army. His luck was still in, for he was treated as an equal, wined and dined in the officers' mess, and quartered with the Vichy officers. It was not a bad way to become a POW, but Bradford could not get on with his escape, even though he was told he would be moved to Marseilles, and thence back to England. Some other British military were also held by the same unit and told to expect to be shipped south and then repatriated. As time went by, however, it seemed fairly certain that in the end fugitive British soldiers and airmen would end up back in either a German prison camp or one run by the Vichy French government.

It was time to get moving again.

Bradford and other fugitives got considerable assistance from the American Quakers, who helped them further on their way south. But no amount of help from them or friendly French could help them on the road, in casual encounters with suspicious civilians, or with routine questioning by a German patrol or Vichy police. Down here, the favored line was to say they were Belgian—that helped account for what was ugly French to a Frenchman, and it was far enough south that most ordinary people tended to be unsure about what Belgian French really sounded like.

With the Spanish border now not far away, another problem arose. Bradford spoke no Spanish and was composing a very short list of critical phrases he would try to learn, things like "I am hungry" or "I am thirsty," together with a fairly comprehensive list of basic foods. Later on, entertained by Spaniards, he would try some of his canned phrases, to the intense amusement of his hosts.

Bradford had another close call right on the border, when in company with a friendly French doctor who was trying to lead him and another officer into position to make a rush across the Spanish frontier. Bradford had sold his bicycle by now so they were on foot, but there were still customs police and *gardes mobiles* to avoid.

The long-awaited attempt to cross the border through the Pyrenees came on August 3 and was a bitter disappointment. The climb was miserable, up to altitudes above 9,000 feet and down again . . . right into the arms of a party of Spanish Civil Guards. The situation still seemed promising, however, as the British fugitives were well treated and the police plan seemed to be—as far as they understood it—to pass them on deeper into Spain, to Saragosa, which was exactly what they wanted.

Instead, it was back to France again. Bernard was imprisoned but took the opportunity to "borrow" an official stamp while in the commandant's office and make himself a pass. That got him a couple of days of freedom, until he ran into some over-inquisitive policemen and ended up in still another concentration camp.

Undeterred, Bradford made himself a rope of sheets and climbed out the latrine window in the dark. It was a leap of faith in a very real sense, since he was without any accurate idea of whether his improvised rope would reach the ground. It didn't. While he was out on his rope pondering whether to drop the rest of the way, the occupant of a bedroom level with Bradford looked out, saw him, and raised the alarm.

Bradford found that he had the misfortune to run out of rope opposite the bedroom of the prison commandant. He dropped off his rope and reached the ground safely, but was run down by guard personnel before he could clear the barbed wire around the camp's perimeter.

Back to the slammer.

Within a few days, a visiting general announced that the prisoners would be sent home, and until arrangements were made they could leave the prison "on parole." Parole was all very well, but Bradford and several other British soldiers were still in France and eager to get home. The first step was a return to Marseilles, where a number of British fugitives were hidden. Bradford had perfected his talent for cutting official stamps out of linoleum, so he was able to keep himself well supplied with the official documents so beloved of the European bureaucracy of the day. Now the problem was finding a way out.

How about a boat, somebody suggested, and money-raising proceeded apace. That had produced a plan to board a boat that would carry 150 men or so, but the criminals who were to produce the ship went south with the money and nobody got out. The British confined the three leading gangsters for three days in barracks (on bread and water) but ultimately settled for ordinary prosecution. The Vichy French had long wanted the three behind bars and gave them three years to contemplate their sins.

And so the escapers had a sort of revenge . . . but nobody had gotten out to Britain. Bradford and several other men managed to board a ship for Algiers. The trip was difficult, dodging repeated searches of the ship, penned up in a hull sometimes too hot to touch. Once in Algiers, Bradford and his comrades searched for some friendly contact . . . in vain. The city was crawling with police agents and informants, and again they were arrested.

As usual, the big thing was to avoid admitting they were British military, and all the police got from them was gibberish. That was enough to stave off immediate return to confinement, at least, and gave Bradford and a friend the chance to get to Oran. Once there, he was arrested again, and this time the French police found on him a paper indicating he was a British citizen, plus identification as Polish and French. The police inspector questioned him endlessly, and this time the "I'm Belgian" defense would not work.

Bradford ended up spending two and a half days in a cell two yards by four, together with a contact, a Frenchman, two Germans, nineteen Arabs, and a vast array of voracious insects whose main interest was eating people. He was then moved to another jail with more room but no fewer lice, which Bradford said he could see "coming for you in little lines." Ultimately, they were released but shipped back to Algiers, which to them was exactly the wrong direction.

Then, in March, Bradford appeared before a three-man board that evaluated his physical condition, with an eye toward repatriation. Hope soared, but then crashed again when somebody decided the membership of the board had not been properly constituted and it was all to do over again.

Bradford had "trained" for both examinations by discontinuing any treatment that would help a previously injured leg and soaking the leg daily in cold water. Its obviously atrophied state and the absence of any reaction from the nerves in the calf got Bradford approved for repatriation. For another officer, somewhat healthier, the trick was managed by a friendly French doctor, who administered some of what Bradford called "sick-making" medicine.

Bradford was having other problems, too. He had a recurrence of a sort of dysentery that had attacked him long before, in both the Sudan and India. Now he came down with "gastric influenza and jaundice," which put him in an Algiers nursing facility. He had been in and out of a rich variety of jails and watched luckier comrades get away, he had tried nearly everything, including a wild plan to purloin a French airliner and fly it to friendly territory, which came reasonably close to success.

And there was also mounting depression at being so close to freedom; he had been captured nearly a year earlier and was ready to try anything to have a chance to get back to England.

Including a long, hazardous voyage. In a midget sailboat.

The little boat, *L'Odetic*, was only seventeen feet long, and her crew—Bradford and two other escapers—were far from expert sailors. One, a local named Botton, had never been on a boat before, and Bradford and the third man were rank amateurs. Bradford's whole seagoing experience was two days' sailing small boats; the third man had about the same pitiful time on the bounding main.

They started their escape voyage by running into several other boats while still in the harbor, and capped that dismal performance by getting the mainsail jammed partway up. Once they got a few basics worked out, the three pressed on into a wind that got stronger and stronger until they were bailing steadily.

The whole idea was to sail from North Africa up to Spain, to someplace from which they could get on to Britain in some semblance of safety. But first they had to master this frustrating business of sailing their creaking antique of a vessel, bailing constantly, drenched by heavy seas so cold they were shivering. The first night at sea was not encouraging.

The next day was a bit brighter, with a somewhat more manageable sea and enough sun to dry out both the escapers and their meager store of rations. Bradford and his companions plucked up enough courage to rig an oar as an improvised jib boom, and their speed increased accordingly.

Their unhandy boat labored, however, for the cables that controlled their centerboard (like a keel, to ye landlubbers) were frayed, and would stand little pressure. Finally, the centerboard banged and hammered so badly that to avoid damage they had to retract it, which further degraded the stability of the boat.

Even so, they made progress north, and hope began to revive again. On the fourth day, however, their favorable breeze fell away, and the excellent progress they had made until then declined to nearly nothing. They were passed by a ship one night, so closely they could hear men talking on board, but there was no hail, no challenge. Progress was further hindered by the ineptitude of Botton, whose adventures in steering sometimes got them pointed in the wrong direction. Botton was later succinctly described by Bradford as a "Communist and rather a useless man."

And at last, after a week at sea, they raised a lighthouse, and guessed from its relative brilliance and the pattern of its flashes that it was at Ceuta, on the Spanish coast. And at last they saw a boat sailing toward them and Bradford put on his tie, the better to "argue with a Spaniard." But then a British voice hailed, "Is that Captain Bradford?"

And in that moment they knew they were safe.

They were formally asked for permission to come aboard by a beautifully uniformed young officer, and transported to his ship, once a luxury yacht named *Sayonara*, and on that incongruous note the long, long odyssey at last came to an end.

The totals are impressive: in round figures: 374 days, 600 miles walking, 500 more by bicycle, 2,500 miles by train and other vehicles, 470 miles by ship, and 700 miles in a small boat.

Bradford, ever the professional, went back to the war—with the Scots, of course—and in time rose to command a battalion of the Black Watch. Postwar, he held a series of other important posts until his retirement in June of 1959 as an honorary brigadier. He finished as a member of the British Empire, holding a Military Cross, two awards of the Distinguished Service Medal, and a Mention in Despatches. He died in 1996, just a little short of his eighty-fourth birthday.

CHAPTER ELEVEN

Twelve Iron Men

WHEN THE JAPANESE TIDE ROLLED OVER THE PHILIPPINES IN 1942, thousands of people became prisoners. They were American and Filipino, military and civilian, men and women, children too. Those who survived the horrors of the Bataan Death March and the brutality and illness of foul prisons like Cabanatuan or Bilibid hungered first for news of their loved ones, of the outside, of home and the free world, and second, for a way to return to that world. From the distant Philippines, neither desire was easy to fill.

Especially was this so for veterans of the Death March, none of whom would ever forget that ordeal, the prisoners tied to trees along the march route and bayoneted, the deliberate deprivation of food and, worse, water, the smug infliction of whatever indignity pleased the Japanese, from exhaustion to hunger to thirst to foul latrine trenches crawling with maggots. Many prisoners were forced to defecate in their own clothing; they dared not halt. One prisoner counted twenty-seven decapitated fellow prisoners along the march route before he quit counting.

Nobody would ever forget the brief rain shower, a gift from heaven, a chance to get a little moisture in their bodies, a little coolness on their filthy, weary skin. The marches, the cruelty, and the trips in stinking, crowded freight cars so hot you couldn't touch the side had one other beneficial effect on many men: hatred, deep and lasting. That emotion made many prisoners stronger in the midst of misery; they would live to take revenge, not for themselves so much as for all the dead men who littered the line of those ghastly marches. It would be years before Japan reaped the whirlwind of her own sowing, but when that wind came, it would be terrible beyond belief.

A strange interlude came when prisoners were transported part of the way to Davao, their ultimate destination, in a ship, a little eight-knot clunker called—of all things—the *Erie Maru*. But—and this was a large *but*—the little vessel was run by the Japanese Imperial Navy, not the army, and the treatment of the prisoners was humane, even kind. The food was clean and palatable; one sick prisoner was carried up on deck near the captain's cabin. He was frequently visited by the captain himself and surrounded with little gifts from the crew—cigarettes, food, even a bowl of flowers.

Davao camp was, however, the same old thing, an army-run hole, dirty and brutal, which did nothing to reconcile the prisoners to Japanese captivity, nothing to dissipate the intense desire to escape. This is the story of twelve men, ten American prisoners of war and two Filipino civil prisoners, murderers at that, who managed the impossible: an escape from the Japanese-occupied Philippines. Their achievement would have been a monumental feat at any time; it was especially so in the spring of 1943, when the islands had long been Japanese occupied.

The escapers were all extraordinary men, who planned long and carefully to escape and reach friendly soil. Major Ed Dyess, veteran fighter pilot; Steve Mellnik, USAAF major; Jack Hawkins, first lieutenant, Marines; Paul Marshall, U.S. Army sergeant; fighter pilot Sam Grashio, first lieutenant; second lieutenant Leo Boelens, a mechanical genius engaged in getting unflyable planes aloft; U.S. Navy Lieutenant-Commander Melvyn McCoy, the senior officer; Mike Dobervich, also a Marine "first balloon"; Robert Spielman, U.S. Army sergeant and bosom buddy of Marshall; Austin Shofner (called "Shifty"), Marine captain; and the two Filipinos, Ben de la Cruz and Victor Jumarong. De la Cruz was an experienced pharmacist and first-aid man; Jumarong was his friend. Not only would Ben not leave without Victor, but Victor was said to know the trail across the morass of swamp and mud that surrounded the camp and made movement very difficult.

Chaplain Richard Carberry had been one of the original group but elected to stay behind to minister to the religious needs of the rest of the prisoners. He gave his life for his parishioners, dying in 1945 on the *Brazil Maru*, a foul prison ship bound for Japan, of wounds suffered in bombing by friendly aircraft; he was buried at sea along with many others.

Carberry was not alone. To the everlasting disgrace of the Japanese leaders, the unmarked prison ships were not only the worst of foul, cramped living conditions but also sitting ducks for Allied aircraft and submarines. There is some indication that the Allies knew the prison ships were among the convoys they attacked; it may well be so, but since the prison ships were unmarked, the sub skippers and aircraft pilots had no choice.

Being veteran military men, the Davao escapers knew the need to prepare, for they faced a long, hard march through brutal country, an ordeal for hungry, tired men even without pursuing Japanese. But between them they had a wealth of talent and no end of pure daring. They began accumulating canned food, mostly bartered for with the standard prison currency, cigarettes.

Dyess managed to be alone in the little compound hospital long enough to snag water purification tablets, a quart jug of quinine pills, and a kit containing not only the usual iodine and dressings but also invaluable sulfa drugs. Dobervich had a compass, kept since he was captured, and Hawkins still had his wristwatch. McCoy set Hawkins's watch and figured its variation based on a formula found in an old copy of *Ripley's Believe It or Not*.

In the navigation area, McCoy had torn out and secreted navigation tables and Mellnik contributed a book on astronomy, which he used to compute and compile data for navigation. Boelens, working from a picture in *Webster's Dictionary*, contrived a homemade sextant and stole tools from the machine shop while Sam Grashio purloined matches from the kitchen.

To Hawkins fell the task of getting the all-important bolo knives, essential to any progress at all where they were going. He enlisted the aid of an elderly Filipino, who finally delivered three bolos, complete with carved wooden sheaths. It was beautiful work, and Hawkins offered to pay for the knives out of their carefully hoarded store of money. The Filipino said, "No, no money." He only wanted one thing. "You kill Japs!"

The escapers didn't ignore the absolute necessity of breaking out in the best physical shape possible. That meant food, of course, far beyond the miserable rations of the camp. There was a plan for that, too. Food was obviously a major concern at all times; even the Japanese funeral offerings for a dead guard were fair game. The cakes, rice, and meat disappeared to feed the friendly; and the rest was, in Dyess's words, "the first beer I had had in many a day."

Operation Chicken provided the best sustenance. Out beyond the fields of coffee where the prisoners labored was the compound chicken coop, where thousands of hens were kept, busy producing eggs and tasty meat additions to the guards' rice. Trouble was, the coop was surrounded by barbed wire, and a guard tower loomed above it. Careful reconnaissance, revealed, however, that the single sentry was given to a midday nap, and when he took it, a highly efficient team of chicken thieves and egg robbers went quickly to work.

The team "coordinator" orchestrated the hen-napping and egg-grabbing, while the "snatcher" actually did the deed. Another man, the "watcher," maintained surveillance over the single avenue of escape, and the "guard-sitter's" job was to warn of a guard's approach. The team had a set of simple hand signals, and once inside the snatcher was signaled by pebbles tossed onto the roof of the coop; a handful of pebbles thrown together translated as "run like hell." The poultry raids were risky but essential. The escapers correctly reasoned that there was no use escaping if they broke down on the trail outside from physical weakness.

Chicken-raiding had its risks, not least the concerted squawking of dozens of irate hens or the ever-present danger of wandering guards. There were several narrow escapes, but the system worked. The escapers were well fed: They got away with 133 hens in three months. Japanese suspicions were aroused about the time chicken number 75 disappeared, but they never solved the mystery. In their frustration, they did indulge in some typically Japanese antics. They withheld chicken feed in some sort of weird retaliation for the disappearing hens and the drop in egg supply. Such an action was not entirely surprising: They had been known to beat vehicle engines that would not start.

The final prisoner coup was the recruiting of Filipino friend Pop Abrina to help. It was not easy. Pop would not even speak to them for several days after the plot was revealed, and then he denounced the escape as a pipe dream, an impossibility; there was the swamp, the headhunters, the Japanese. But then he slowly came around, in part lured by the thought of reward for him.

"Well," said McCoy, "we have influence in high places," and Mellnik had in fact worked for General MacArthur. They could promise nothing, of course, but the chance was enough. Pop was on board, and the escape had acquired a very good asset indeed, a daring man whom even the guards called "*tomodachi*"—friend—entertained by his banter and his tales of sexual conquest.

Davao "penal colony" was not only covered by the usual force of guards, but surrounded by a virtually impenetrable swamp, a gooey morass that stretched on for some twenty miles in every direction. There was life in the swamp all right, but most of it was of the mosquito and crocodile variety, except for wandering bands of natives, whose tasty habit was collecting people's heads. The locals believed the swamp had a malignant personality all its own. Maybe it did.

Certainly the camp's guard force did. Rumor had it that the deputy commandant, one Hozumi, had somehow disgraced himself in combat, and he and his guards took out his shame on the prisoners. The food was terrible and entirely insufficient, 600 grams a day for the hardest work, for men worked far too hard and were afflicted with a whole panoply of exotic diseases, most of which were not fixable.

But for the escape club, things gradually improved, helped along for them and the rest by the providential arrival of long-overdue Red Cross parcels, two per prisoner, a total of thirty pounds of good things. They came toward the end of January 1943 and got through even though the Japanese had stolen some of the contents. Both health and morale improved dramatically.

The escapers continued their scrounging and planning. Assuming they got through Dismal Swamp and evaded the Japanese, the plan was to press on to the east coast of Mindanao, striking it at about the town of Cateel. That was a difficult trip of some sixty miles, but worse was to come. After that, the plan called for larceny of a boat seaworthy enough to sail a mere 1,300 miles to Australia. Navigation would necessarily be by dead reckoning, with whatever help the improvised sextant could provide, but the formidable McCoy thought it could be done. He wanted, however, a crew of at least nine, providing three three-man watches.

A new sense of urgency drove the plotters. What if, they wondered, the Japanese thought of instituting the "shooting squad" plan? That nasty Japanese mechanism, already in effect elsewhere, meant simply that if a man escaped, the other members of his squad would be automatically executed. Nobody was willing to sacrifice other prisoners for his own freedom, so that would put an end to thoughts of escape. There was reason to hurry.

And so an excuse for Sunday labor was invented. The Marines already went out on Sunday to change the grazing ground for the bulls they had charge of; that was routine. The others—assigned as coffee pickers—told the Japanese they wanted to build a rain shelter because too many of them were getting sick. Since this Sunday work would not interfere with routine coffee-bean picking and a healthier crew would obviously speed production, the Japanese agreed.

The escapers carefully studied and chose their route. The road was out; too many Japanese used it too often, which left either the railroad cut or a faint, abandoned trail. The trail was chosen, overgrown though it surely was, wandering though it did, because it was obscure and because it came out of the swamp some twenty miles away near a village called Lungaog. The invaluable Victor knew the way. There they might find help, even contact with the Philippine Resistance.

Two serious dangers the escape had to weather, with only a couple of weeks to go before getaway day. Busily stealing onions from the prison patch, Hawkins and Dobervich were accosted by a furious American officer and "disciplined" by the camp senior officer for breaking the Japanese rules. They were pulled from the plowing detail, but within days their sentences were "commuted," thanks to intervention by friends with enough rank to matter.

The last moments of preparation were the hardest. Dyess took the biggest risk, driving his buffalo cart to the departure point with a last load of escape gear concealed under stacks of saplings—"fence posts," to the guards he had to pass. He made it, thanks to his small kindnesses to the guards over many weeks; they all knew him and nobody thought to search his cart any longer.

Almost worse was what befell Grashio and Shofner: They had made a rare slip and were caught by Hozumi enjoying bananas, what the furious Japanese officer called the "fruit of the Japanese empire!" Some slapping and punching followed, but the worst moment came when one guard searched Shofner's musette bag, presumably looking for more of the imperial bananas. He missed the bottle of quinine, discovery of which would have sunk the whole enterprise and meant the death of both Americans.

They weren't out of the woods yet. The Japanese decided on mass punishment for the despicable crime of eating the emperor's bananas. On the Sunday appointed for the break, everybody was ordered to work in the rice paddies. There was nothing for it but to delay their break another week. It was high time to go, for incidents of brutality against the prisoners were on the rise. One prisoner had been shot to death for no good reason by a tower guard, and the army lieutenant colonel in charge of the sugarcane-cutting crew was tied to a stake and badly beaten for twenty-four hours. His heinous crime was trying to bring some sugarcane to patients in the hospital . . . presumably imperial sugarcane.

But the next Sunday dawned with the escape still not revealed, and the escapers packed a few precious trinkets and useful items and dressed for the run. They passed the guards on their way to "work" and linked up with Jumarong and de la Cruz, although both of them were late. Then it was the swamp trail and the great adventure.

The path was gloomy and overgrown, "as dark," in a favorite GI phrase, "as the inside of your hat." The Filipinos led the way, and it soon became apparent that if Jumarong once knew the trail, he'd lost it now. And so the little party went to Plan B, a vague and difficult trip to the northeast to try to hit the Japanese logging railway. The going was very hard indeed, but one bright spot there was: instead of fiddling with water purification tables and stagnant swamp water, the Filipinos showed them the magic of the *buhuka* vine, which bloated itself with sweet, safe water and was easy to find.

Back at the camp, the Japanese were puzzled and furious, counting and recounting prisoners, and always coming up short. There were all manner of threats, and nobody could guess whether the "shooting squads" would suddenly appear. Rumor and Japanese curses and threats flew through the camp. One Japanese interpreter known to the prisoners as "Running Wada" delivered an ominous oration, grim for all that it was missing the ever-elusive "L": "For every man who escape, de other nine in his squad wirr be shoot kirred. You are arr guilty of herping them escape."

And a great deal more of the same twaddle. There also were threats to execute the men who slept next to the vanished prisoners, and all of this blustering was threatening enough when it was delivered. In the event, there was no shooting of squad members, although the new American camp commander and the leaders of the escapers' barracks were severely beaten up.

The escapers were clear so far but moving very slowly, sometimes no more than three or four hundred yards in an hour, hacking their way through masses of trees and vines, knee-deep and deeper in water, pushing through huge clumps of *cogon*, a species of monstrous sword grass that ripped and tore skin and cloth at the slightest contact. Finally, they halted in the accompanying cloud of mosquitos to discover they were traveling in circles. Regrouping, they pushed on, in spite of the fact that everybody was exhausted, McCoy was feeling symptoms of an onset of malaria, and they had to spend a half-hour immersed in the foul swamp water to shelter from a cloud of large, angry wasps.

About at the bottom of their resources, they heard gunfire—single shots and automatic weapons. The weapons were not all Japanese, either, and the fight, whatever it was, could have been as near as a mile. The fighting told the escapers that direction was not one to take hastily. Instead, they halted briefly while Grashio led them in prayer, and a great calm descended on them all. Grashio knew what had happened: "I thought a miracle had occurred. I felt now that God would save us."

In short order, the exhausted Americans began to encounter fewer clumps of sword grass and shallower water. At last Jumarong found a trail and they soon arrived at the railroad; it looked like the Promised Land. It looked even better when they stumbled into a village and were warmly welcomed by the inhabitants. The escapers were fed a delicacy called a *baloot*, which is a chicken or duck egg, including a partially formed chick in a sort of jelly. It would have been impolite to refuse.

It got even better when they were confronted by a Filipino guerrilla sergeant named Casiano de Juan, hung all over with deadly weapons. After making sure the escapers weren't Japanese spies, he announced that "we are happy to see Americans." "Big boy," said Dyess, "we're a helluva lot happier to see you." From that moment on, to both Americans and guerrillas, Casiano de Juan would be forever-after "Big Boy."

Big Boy whistled, at which fifty-odd ragged guerrillas emerged from the shrubbery and a general welcome and celebration followed. In the general conversation that followed, it developed that the firefight heard by the escapers had been Casiano's boys ambushing a Japanese force apparently following the escapers. Guerrilla lookouts had seen "ten tall white men" followed by "Hapon" soldiers and drawn the right conclusions. The ambush had been a clean guerrilla victory, ten to nothing.

The escapers stayed on with the villagers, made over and fed as often as they wanted to eat. The Americans could wash themselves and their clothing, sleep as long as they chose. There was endless talk, and visitors from nearby villages came to see the Americans; Shofner exhibited photos he had taken on Corregidor and back in Shanghai and the Americans told tales of the Japanese horror. There was a plenteous supply of *tuba*, a sort of white lightning made from the coconut palm. Some villagers even asked the visitors to stand as godparents to their children.

The happy time ended when a Filipino sergeant appeared with an invitation from his captain, Laureta, and the escapers set off to see him, their progress a sort of traveling fiesta. There was music and dancing, and everybody sang, including the Americans. One evening ended with the Filipinos singing "God Bless America," and the Americans responding with "God Bless the Philippines."

They were passed on to the Filipino captain, who made them welcome and asked their advice. He showed them a letter purporting to be from U.S. Army Lieutenant-Colonel Ernest McClish, who wrote that he commanded a substantial guerilla force and invited Laureta to join him. "I'd like to," said the captain, but he was afraid the letter was a Japanese ruse; they had tried to lure him into an ambush before. It's no hoax, said Mellnik, who knew McClish personally, at which Laureta asked whether the Americans would handle the contact with him. They would.

And so plans changed. Cateel town was a week's march away and McClish's headquarters somewhat farther, a tough hike over jungle and river and mountain; it was also headhunter country. The Americans felt they owed Laureta, however, who said he would help them out with their original escape plan if they could not reach McClish. And then there was a very interesting line in McClish's letter that said he had radio contact with Australia.

The expedition to find McClish departed with a strong guerrilla escort, and for a while Laureta led it. He turned back partway, and one of his lieutenants took over. The headhunters failed to materialize and finally, in a village called Loreto, they came upon a magic sight, an American flag hanging from what passed for city hall. At last they met another American *guerrillero*, Lieutenant Walter Mester, who passed them on to Captain Tom Baxter, who gave them directions to a place called Medina, where they would find McClish. Since only Shofner and McCoy had useful shoes by now, they became the messengers.

Another arduous trip got them to McClish's "division headquarters." Their reception was frosty at first, until McClish became convinced they were really escapers and bade them and Laureta's lieutenant a hearty welcome. It was *tuba* time. McClish turned out to be a thorough professional, an Oklahoma Choctaw who presided over a ragtag collection of fighters whose strength fluctuated from day to day. They were tough, however, and sufficiently organized to have their own newspaper, print their own money, even modify vehicles to run on the omnipresent *tuba*. Besides the Filipino guerrillas, there were many Americans from all the services, a number of civilians, and even a handful of British and other nationalities.

McClish immediately started promoting everybody. Probably the biggest jump was elevating the two Filipinos to sergeant from convicted-killer-serving-life. Later, Mellnik would travel to a New York sanitarium to have dying Philippine president Manuel Quezon sign formal pardons for de la Cruz and Jumarong.

The two American NCOs suddenly blossomed as second lieutenants. Everybody else got a one-grade jump, the Marines magically becoming officers in both the Marine Corps and the army. All that now remained was getting home, and that would be tough enough. There was more arduous travel, although now they were in the company of both Filipino and American fighting men. Part of the journey to salvation was by water, part by land. But in the end, the plain evidence of salvation, the final miracle, was the rushing emergence of a U.S. Navy submarine from the depths beside their small boat.

There were three such miracles, in July, September, and November of 1943, as the *Trout*, *Bowfin*, and *Narwhal*, alerted by radio, carried the escapers far out of harm's way. Dyess, Mellnik, and McCoy were first out, exhaustively questioned by intelligence personnel on their return but unable to get a national audience for their accounts of the almost unimaginable brutality of the Japanese.

Grashio boarded USS *Bowfin* in September of 1943, torn by conflicting emotions. He ached to see his country again, but he was deeply grieved to be leaving his friend Leo Boelens. Boelens could have returned to the States on *Bowfin* but chose to remain in the Philippines to organize construction of an airfield in the middle of nowhere, an alleged 1.4-million square-foot monster. It would never be finished, for the Japanese caught up with him, shot him, and then stabbed him brutally and repeatedly.

He had lived only a month longer than Ed Dyess, who had gone back to his beloved fighters. Nobody knows precisely what happened, but although Dyess was an experienced pilot, he was flying the twin-engined P-38, very hot and new to him, and seems to have ignored at least part of his preflight check. As he took off for the first time, one engine began to backfire, probably the result of the low-test fuel used in training. But instead of braking, he tried to take off, the missing of the engine growing ever worse. Dyess reached about 200 feet, his wheels still down, slowing the fighter's speed still further.

Dyess, being the sort of man he was, would not bail out and let the P-38 crash into a crowded residential area. Instead, he tried to put the plane down on an empty street, but when a car unexpectedly drove below him, he changed direction to get the airplane down on a small vacant lot. It was in vain, and after all the risks and all the miles, Ed Dyess died instantly in the fighter's wreckage. It was three days before Christmas 1943.

Narwhal surfaced at a place called Nasipit and found a carnival atmosphere waiting. As she docked at the local pier, her crew was greeted by a guerrilla band's version of "The Stars and Stripes Forever" and the sight of kegs of beer and roasted pig. As workers unloaded supplies destined for the guerillas, the band shifted over to "The Eyes of Texas" and "Yankee Doodle." Sailors raided their lockers, throwing the local people clothing, candy, and cigarettes. Dobervich tossed his shoes to a shoeless Filipino; Shofner gave his BAR — Browning Automatic Rifle — to McClish: "Big Boy will need this back."

And when the celebration was done and the farewells said, *Narwhal* pushed out to sea, carrying not only Dobervich, Shofner, and Hawkins but also thirty-some evacuees. The group included several women and children and at least one baby.

The story of the Philippine prison-camp horror had been suppressed by the government far too long, but it broke finally on Friday, January 29, 1944. The tales that Dyess, Mellnik, and

McCoy had told so many months before were suddenly all over the papers and magazines. America was furious. "The American emotion," said *Newsweek*, "was a fury such as had never before gripped the nation in this war."

That the fury broke, even as late as it did, owed much to the gallantry and spirit of twelve men. The men who had died in Japanese captivity would be avenged.

In spades.

CHAPTER TWELVE

Come What May

"WHEELS UP!" CAPTAIN PETER PROSSEN SHOUTED JUST BEFORE handing the Gremlin Special over to his copilot George Nicholson for the joyride to "Shangri-La," a picturesque valley smack-dab in the middle of New Guinea, with nine women from the Women's Army Corps (WAC) aboard. They were leaving the Sentani air field near the Allied base at Hollandia.

Nicholson had degrees from Boston College, Boston University, and Harvard but had been a pilot only about three years. Neither Prossen nor Nicholson had flown to Shangri-La before. After a few minutes, Prossen joined his guests in the cabin. This particular trip was an appreciation gift to his hard-working staff. One of the WACs joined Nicholson in the cabin for a better view.

One hour later, Nicholson dropped the C-47 into the canyon so steeply that it was impossible to gradually climb high enough to clear the cliff that guarded the entrance to their destination. He did the only thing possible, pulling the control wheel back quickly. Seconds became minutes as the Gremlin struggled for altitude. John McCollum, himself a pilot along for the ride with his twin brother, Robert, knew instinctively that Nicholson was flying blind through a low-lying cloudbank. "This is gonna be close," McCollum had yelled, but it wasn't.

Whether Nicholson had simply dropped the plane too low or it had been pushed down by a sudden downdraft as an official report later suggested, the result was the same. The Gremlin began peeling the tops off of jungle evergreens just before crashing against the mountain and exploding.

New Guinea was and is an inhospitable, sparsely populated place alien to most Westerners. Yet a thousand languages, about one-sixth of all languages in the world, are spoken here among the natives, some of whom are cannibals. New Guinea is largely invisible to twenty-first-century civilization. The island was most recently newsworthy when Michael Rockefeller, the fifth and last child of former U.S. vice-president Nelson Rockefeller, disappeared in New Guinea under mysterious circumstances in November 1961. In the years since, some researchers have speculated that Rockefeller was killed by natives in revenge for an incident involving the Dutch three years earlier. After all, relations between the Europeans and the New Guinea natives have been tumultuous since the very beginning.

In 1526, Portuguese explorer Jurge de Meneses observed the westernmost part of the island from a distance and named it Papua. Twenty years later, the Spanish explorer Inigo Ortiz de Retes called it New Guinea because the natives resembled natives he'd seen in Guinea, Africa.

Europeans divided and redivided New Guinea in the centuries that followed. When World War II began, the Dutch ruled the western half of the island from their capital at Hollandia on the northern coast. Japan invaded New Guinea in 1942, hoping to use it as a staging area for later attacks on Australia, some thousand miles away. Operation Reckless conducted in April 1944 reclaimed Hollandia. MacArthur commanded Allied forces from a massive two-story headquarters he had built there, setting the stage for his eventual return to the Philippines. The Far East

Air Command headquarters provided supply, logistics, and maintenance for Allied forces flying against the Japanese forces across the Pacific battlefront from Hollandia.

Margaret Hastings, a Women's Army Corps volunteer from Oswego, New York, arrived in Hollandia just in time for Christmas that year. She worked as a secretary for Colonel Prossen, a pilot serving as chief of the maintenance section of the Far East Air Service Command, doing the type of work she had previously done for the Remington Rand Company factory at Oswego. Margaret was a striking beauty who drank liquor and liked boys, "but not too much." New Guinea was no vacation spot, as one writer pointed out. The coastal areas featured swamps and jungles; the often hostile inhabitants of the interior chose between between limestone mountains and dense rain forests.

Hollandia was eventually designated "the worst place in the war for the health of military women." The hapless occupants reported spiders the size of coffee saucers, all five known types of jungle rot, and a climate that made New Guinea a paradise for fungus.

That May, in the last year of the war, Japanese forces still skulked about in the jungles and forests of New Guinea, some eighteen miles away. Yet boredom had been the real enemy until Major Myron Grimes and Colonel Ray T. Elsmore, commander of the 322nd Troop Carrier Wing stationed at Hollandia, had discovered a sightseeing diversion thirteen months earlier. He had been searching for a clearing that might serve as an airstrip midway between Hollandia and the Allied base at Merauke on the northern and southern coasts. Grimes and Elsmore had reported discovering a mysterious uncharted tabletop valley some 150 air miles from Hollandia that seemed to be a good prospect.

There was one major problem. Just as Grimes and Elsmore dropped their Lockheed C-60 transport plane into the valley,

Elsmore spotted a sheer cliff looming in the distance. "Push on," Grimes urged, meaning that rather than steeply climbing out of the valley, Elsmore should climb just enough to clear the terrain and see what was beyond the cliff. In a few seconds, the pilots were both stunned:

> *Safely in the clear, Elsmore saw a break in the puffy clouds, framing the vista like a heavenly vision. Spread out before them was a place their maps said didn't exist, a rich valley Elsmore later called a "riot of dazzling color." The land was largely flat, giving him a clear view of its full breadth— nearly thirty miles long and more than eight miles wide at its widest point, running northwest to southeast. Surrounding the valley were sheer mountain walls with jagged ridges running to the clouds.*
>
> *At the southeastern end, a river entered the valley by cascading over a cliff. The cocoa-colored river, more than a hundred feet wide in spots, snaked through the valley, interrupted by occasional rapids. At the valley's northwestern end, the river disappeared into an enormous hole in the mountain wall that formed a natural grotto, its upper arch some three hundred feet above the ground. Much of the valley was carpeted by tall, sharp kunai grass, waist-high in spots, interrupted by occasional stands of trees.*
>
> *Even more remarkable than the valley's physical splendor were it inhabitants: tens of thousands of people for whom the Stone Age was the present day.*

Grimes called the place Hidden Valley. Later, in official reports, Elsmore named it Baliem for the river, which entered the south end of the valley in a cascading waterfall. One of the several hundred villages Elsmore and Grimes observed was called Uwambo.

Soon, Elsmore showed the Hidden Valley to two reporters, George Lait and Harry Patterson, who renamed it in separate articles published in March and April 1944.

They called it Shangri-La.

James Hilton first coined the term in his 1933 novel *Lost Horizon*, brought to the screen four years later by the legendary producer and director Frank Capra. The Shangri-La of fiction was a mystical, harmonious place free from conflict and violence.

Elsmore soon began promoting the "Shangri-La Society." He devised a parchment certificate awarded to journalists, top brass, and everyone else who had seen the valley on C-47 tours. From the air, one native village resembled an irregularly shaped "E" complete with thirty-foot watchtowers. The valley was virtually inaccessible, since C-47 transports and other military aircraft would sink to their wheels in the soft uneven ground. Shangri-La was also surrounded by hostile natives and Japanese soldiers.

The Elsmore-conducted Shangri-La tours had become commonplace by Mother's Day, May 13, 1945. In Connecticut, the *Hartford Courant* feature an article titled "Pacific Reporter: Shangri-La" that very morning as Colonel Prossen prepared for yet another routine paradise flyover. Margaret Hastings was invited at the last minute, almost as an afterthought. She hurried through her work and a chicken-and-ice cream lunch many GIs would have envied to make the plane at 2 p.m. She quickly sat next to fellow WACs Laura Besley and Eleanor Hanna in the very last seats on board in the next-to-last back-row seat on the left. Few, if any, wore seat belts.

After the crash, Lieutenant John McCollum from Trenton, Mississippi, had been knocked to the cabin floor near the back of the plane. He began looking for a way out and soon found it where the tail section used to be. Hastings was on fire nearby, clutched in the grip of a dead man whose last thought was to protect her from the coming crash. Years later, she recalled almost resigning herself to death, but when it was nearly too late, she pulled herself out of the dead man's arms and crawled toward the light at the back of the plane. She was crawling through a silence interrupted only by the crackling of flame and the smell of flesh and human hair.

"My God, Hastings!" Hastings heard someone say just after she had fallen through the hole at the back of the plane to the ground a few feet below her. Just about then Kenneth Decker, a sergeant from Kelso, Washington, emerged from the right side of the burning plane with a bloody gash in his forehead deep enough to expose dull gray skull bone. His right elbow was broken, he was burned from head to foot, but somehow he kept walking. Today was Decker's thirty-fourth birthday.

"Get me out of here!" Someone had yelled from inside the plane, so now McCollum snaked his way back into the plane until he found Laura Besley, and then returned again for Eleanor Hanna, burned though she was, from head to foot. Hastings and McCollum had just positioned Hanna and Besley a safe distance from the wreck when McCollum heard a man yelling from the front right side of the Gremlin. McCollum and Decker followed the voice until he could see a man in the far distance. It was Captain Herbert Good, a staff officer for General MacArthur whom McCollum had personally invited to join the Shangri-La joyride.

Before Decker and McCollum could reach Captain Good, the plane exploded again. Later, when they examined his body, they discovered that Good's left foot had been anchored to jungle underbrush. He never had a chance to escape.

In the hours that followed, the flames erupted again and again, cremating the twenty-one bodies inside the fuselage, even as Eleanor Hanna tried to raise her voice in song. Years later, a recovery party found only one personally identifiable artifact inside the wreck: a gold wedding ring worn by John McCollum's twin brother, Robert.

As the flames threatened to surround the survivors, Hastings spotted a bare rock ledge with just enough room for the five of them to rest twenty yards down the side of the mountain. She began crawling through the jungle. "Covering its rocky, muddy, uneven floor was a snarling mess of giant ferns, vines, shrubs, fallen tree trunks and spongy mosses, always wet. Thorns and spines and saw-toothed leaves ensnared her legs and tore her clothes and skin."

Worse yet, above her head "was a tumble of trees" containing "gnarled webs of thick woody vines. . . . The lush flora created a luxuriant bouquet, as the jungle carried out its endless cycle of birth, decay, death and new birth."

Arriving first on the ledge, Hastings looked up toward the other survivors. She saw McCollum carrying Eleanor Hanna, a Chinese coin bracelet still hanging from her limp wrist, just before he slipped on the wet jungle trail, fell against a tree, and broke a rib.

McCollum later returned to the plane twice for food, water, and survival gear. On the first trip, he found first-aid supplies, some hard candy, several small tins of water, and two heavy, bright yellow life rafts that seemed useless at the time. On a return visit, McCollum and Decker found two cots, seventeen canteens of water, and more first-aid supplies.

On the morning of Monday, May 14, McCollum rose early and discovered that Eleanor had died during the night, surprising no one. But within eighteen hours, Laura Besley had also died under mysterious circumstances. Although she was burned, the burns were not painful, but she shook continuously, suggesting to McCollum that Laura might have suffered internal injuries. By the early morning hours of May 15, just after midnight, Laura's struggle was over.

Later that morning, McCollum climbed a tree near their rock ledge and spotted a clearing several miles from the crash site. He knew instinctively that a rescue was no sure thing, but they had to try. In November 1942, another C-47, this one called the Flying Dutchman, had also crashed into a New Guinea mountain side; that time, seventeen of the twenty-three aboard survived the crash, but only four made it to an Allied base.

By the day that the Gremlin went down, some six hundred American planes had crashed in New Guinea. Just the month before, the wife of a missing pilot who made inquiries learned about the conditions would-be rescuers faced: "It is necessary to cross high mountain ranges on practically every flight made on the island. Thick jungle growth goes right up to the tops of the peaks and entire squadrons could completely disappear under this foliage." The letter continued: "No matter how thorough the search is, the possibility of locating the plane is rather remote. We have had numerous other instances of like nature and no word has come concerning these crews or airplanes. The weather and terrain account for more [missing] airplanes than combat flying."

McCollum was determined that these survivors, however few, would be different. The clearing was their only hope of being spotted and rescued. Hastings wished later that the surviving three had said a prayer, built a cross, or done something to recognize their twenty-one friends, but they had little choice but to move on if they were to survive.

Since they had been forced to rest on a cliff below the fiery crash, they first had to walk twenty yards back up the mountain to journey toward the clearing. They passed rocky ravines and sheer cliffs where a momentary loss of balance might have meant slow but certain death in the jungle. Almost at the beginning of their descent, Hastings discovered a narrow, often treacherous path downward along a dry creek bed.

From time to time, they were forced to slide or even jump over trees or boulders, resting every half hour to conserve enough strength to move on. They were stopped by a twelve-foot waterfall, but crossed it Indiana Jones style. McCollum crossed the chasm using a heavy vine, threw it back to Hastings who crossed and threw it back. Decker clung to the vine long enough to cross despite the pressure on his shattered elbow. Later, along the way, they found a recent human footprint.

The jungle canopy blocked the sky, but they could hear the airplanes above. The Far East Command had begun looking for them shortly after the Gremlin had missed its estimated arrival time back at the Sentani airfield near Hollandia. Some twenty-four planes began the search, which was made all the more difficult by the lack of accurate maps. Even as the search began, Colonel Elsmore began considering the logistics of mounting a rescue operation if any survivors were spotted from the air.

This would not be simply a matter of dropping in supplies, since the Far East Command assumed from the beginning that some of the survivors would be injured. The initial drops of supplies must be followed by medics and paratroopers. But how would they get them all home?

An overland trek through the jungle was technically feasible but unwise, given the lack of roads and abundance of hostile tribes and Japanese soldiers. Five years later, helicopters might have been a useful option, but the rudimentary choppers then available couldn't fly in the thin altitudes of the mountainous New Guinea interior. They thought about seaplane landings in the Baliem River, PT boats, and even submarines, but in the end the decision came down to paratroopers. The problem was, no paratroopers were available.

McCollum, Hastings, and Decker reached the clearing at about eleven on the morning of Wednesday, May 16. And within minutes they spotted a B-17 Flying Fortress in the clouds above them; when it returned about an hour later, they quickly dragged the bright yellow raft they had found in the plane wreck to a place in the clearing where the plane crew could see them. Captain William D. Baker made a third pass and waggled his wings for them as a Catholic chaplain on board said an impromptu prayer.

But from the shadows beneath the jungle canopy nearby, some cannibals had spotted them too. After the B-17 made that third critical pass, Hastings realized that this clearing was no coincidence or act of nature. The ground had been cleared to grow sweet potatoes, which rested beneath their feet in the tangled undergrowth.

At first, the noise they took for wild dogs barking didn't bother the three survivors. But as it grew louder they began to see dozens of men with axes. Their black, shining bodies glistened in the sun.

The natives confronting them lived in or near Uwambo, one of the villages Grimes and Elsmore had spotted the day Shangri-La was discovered. These natives had two thousand ways to express the word "kill" but worshipped no gods. They only feared their ancestors, who had to be appeased by sacrifices offered near their own designated village huts. Although the warriors did some occasional light gardening for recreation, the men had no occupation other than war. Between wars, the women grew all the food and did all the work, other than building thirty-foot watchtowers at the edges of their villages.

The reasons for these never-ending New Guinea wars were simply unknown. The aborigines believed that by redressing long-forgotten grievances the wars brought balance to life in the jungle and in a sense they did. Centuries ago, the violence had become a form of recreation that perpetually reduced the number of bachelors vying for wives, fostering polygamy.

The natives had, of course, seen airplanes in the skies above their island many times since the Second World War had begun. And some of them had seen the survivors scurrying away from the burning wreckage of the Gremlin on the side of the mountain. But the natives who had seen the crash site didn't know whether the survivors were friends or enemies. And since the leadership in Uwambo often killed messengers bearing bad news, the natives who saw the crash simply remained silent. They didn't know whether the Americans were spirits to be welcomed or enemies to be killed and eaten. The Uwambo people were ceremonial cannibals, who only ate their enemy's hands, unlike their archenemies, the Landikma, who ate everything.

None of this mattered to Hastings when she saw at least forty men emerge from the jungle with "wicked-looking stone axes" and at least one very long spear. The two parties were separated only by a gully. Hastings could only imagine "how awful it would be to survive a plane crash only to end up in a native stew."

"Maybe they'll feed us before they kill us," McCollum quipped, perhaps reaching for his small pocketknife—the only weapon any of them had—before issuing an order. "Smile, damn it!' rasped McCollum.

"We smiled. Oh, we smiled to high heaven." Hastings recalled later. "We smiled for our lives. We smiled and held out the candy and the jackknife and then we waited as the black men advanced."

McCollum and his counterpart across the gully each edged closer to a single log that served as a bridge.

"McCollum reached out and grasped the native's hand. He pumped it like a cross between a politician, a car salesman and a long-lost relative." Wimayuk Wandik, the native leader, whom the Americans promptly nicknamed "Pete," later told his son that the Americans were sky spirits. Whatever their differences, the Americans and the natives shared one impression: These strangers smelled very badly. And at least one of Pete's lieutenants thought that the Americans should be killed on the spot.

Back at the Far East Command, Colonel Elsmore was still looking for paratroopers to mount the rescue operation. And since the survivors had been located, the search was becoming critical. When the rescue operation began, all combat-hardened paratroopers in the area were clearing Japanese soldiers out of the Pacific theater. But John Babcock, a peacetime high school teacher then serving as a staff officer for Colonel Elsmore, had an idea. A few weeks before the Gremlin crashed, Babcock had lunched in the Officers' Club with Captain C. Earl Walter Jr., a former student at the prestigious Black-Foxe Military Institute in Hollywood.

Walter was a fully qualified paratrooper with no prior combat experience sitting out the war in Hollandia when he would rather be fighting. This was no coincidence. His father, C. Earl Walter Sr., was then leading a Resistance force of guerilla fighters in the jungles of Mindanao, the second-largest Philippine island. About six months earlier, when young C. Earl Walter Jr. came ashore at Mindanao in October 1944 to carry out Allied intelligence missions with other paratroopers, his father was waiting with some news. Although there is no documentation proving this, it appears that Walter Sr. thought one Walter risking his life in the Pacific theater at a time was enough. Walter Sr. had arranged with the brass in Washington for his son to sit this one out.

But now Walter the younger developed a different plan. He quickly accepted the assignment, then began deciding which ten men from his largely Filipino First Reconnaissance Battalion would conduct the rescue operation. He needed two medics and eight others willing to take on four distinct challenges. There were no charts, their parachute drop zone was the worst possible place to land, the natives surrounding them were likely to be hostile, and they would have to improvise a path out of the Shangri-La valley through cannibals, headhunters, and Japanese soldiers. Yet everyone volunteered, as several voiced the battalion motto "*Bahala na*": Come what may.

Back in Shangri-La, Hastings, McCollum, and Decker were still starving that Thursday, May 17, the fifth day they had spent in the jungle, sustained only by stale candy and a little water. But now they were in voice contact with Hollandia—thanks to an FM radio dropped into the valley that morning. Although the Far East Command now knew that the others were dead, Hastings asked McCollum not to discuss their wounds, since there was nothing to be done before the supplies and medics arrived.

Later that morning when the trio approached Uwambo, Hastings noticed that the village had a split rail fence straight out the old West. Also, one of the huts had a hole in the roof probably caused by a cargo box. Of more significance, she noted that Decker's wounds were turning gangrenous.

In Hollandia that morning, Captain Walter chose Sergeant Benjamin "Doc" Bulatao and Corporal Camilo "Rammy" Ramirez to carry out the critical medic positions. Ramirez had been on the Bataan Death March but escaped from a Japanese prison by squeezing through a gap in the barbed wire.

The Shangri-La sky above Hastings, Decker, and McCollum filled with cargo-laden parachutes the next morning. The first boxes included pants, shirts, bandages, blankets, and finally, after all that stale candy, canned bacon, ham, eggs, hash, stew, and other delights.

The next morning Doc and Rammy made the treacherous thirty-second jump into Shangri-La. Within two hours they were at the clearing, treating the wounded. And on Sunday, May 20, at 10 a.m., Captain Walter with the rest of his team dropped into the valley some thirty miles wide of the mark right into the middle of a designated aborigine battlefield. One sergeant looked at the two hundred warriors surrounding them and mentioned Custer's Last Stand.

Nobody laughed.

Within hours, they established a base camp. The next morning Captain Walter and five of his men trekked into the jungle but became disoriented and returned to the base camp the morning of May 23. That Thursday, they began hacking a path through the tangled brush and high jungle grass toward the survivors by dead reckoning, using compass directions from their base camp; they slept that night in a slow soaking rain. Captain Walter recorded their despair in his journal. "God only knows where that last ridge is. We can last for a few more days at this rate, but sure as hell [I] would like to know about where we are. Don't like this fooling around without maps." But they had no other choice.

A C-47 somehow found them the next day. Late on the afternoon of Friday, May 25, Hastings heard the distinctive "yapping noise" the natives made when strangers approached. But within minutes, she thought she heard someone singing the latest Andrew Sisters hit, "Shoo Shoo Baby." And she had. Captain Walter came into the clearing, swinging a bolo knife and clearing the trail for the men behind him. Within hours, an American flag was waving over the ten pup tents that Walter called "The Lost Outpost of Shangri-La."

How would they get back to Hollandia? While the rescuers and the survivors played poker and other improvised card games, Captain Walter planned how he would get them out of the jungle. First, however, the dead entangled in what was left of the Gremlin had to be recovered and buried. Funerary supplies were dropped in that Saturday, but several paratroopers sent to find the plane on Sunday had no luck. That Monday, May 27, John McCollum led a burial party back to the mountainside. McCollum's twin brother and the others who could not be identified were placed in a mass grave next to Captain Herbert Good, Sergeant Laura Besley, and Private Eleanor Hanna. Twenty crosses and one Star of David were placed there as Protestant, Catholic, and Jewish chaplains took turns conducting services for the dead by radio.

Back in the United States, Hastings's father, Patrick Hastings, and the other next of kin had barely been notified of the disaster when the newspaper publicity "show" began. Walter Simmons had grown up in Fargo, North Dakota, where his father worked as a patent medicine salesman. He did a flyover with Colonel Elsmore, and then penned a series of articles about Shangri-La for the *Chicago Tribune*, prompting competing articles from the Associated Press, the *Halifax Herald*, and other publications, touting the dangers faced by Margaret Hastings, an authentically beautiful WAC surrounded by cannibals and marooned with no sure means of rescue. This was the sort of story that had long legs, as it were, in the closing days of the war.

As the weeks went by, Captain Walter, eager to see at least some combat, began to grow tired of playing "nursemaid" to the "Queen of Shangri-La," as many in the Far East Command now called Hastings, sometimes for publication. On June 8, he confided a hope to his journal that the mission would open a few people's eyes to the "possibilities of my future plans."

One week later, Doc Bulatao pronounced the three survivors fit for the difficult trek to the paratrooper base camp in the Shangri-La valley. By the time they hiked to the base camp after a difficult three-day walk, Hastings had regained her former strength. She didn't know that her friends among the natives had arranged for her safe passage.

What happened next was entirely unexpected.

Hastings and the others at the Shangri-La base camp knew that documentary filmmaker Alexander Cann was going to parachute into the dense jungle valley, but they didn't know that he was going to be drunk. And this was hardly his first misadventure. The baritone-voiced son of a prominent Canadian banker, Alexander Cann lost his sizable inheritance gambling while in college, regularly drank with film star Humphrey Bogart while working as a character actor in Hollywood, but threw it all away by getting drunk and stealing jewelry worth $96,000 in today's dollars from an ex-wife of William Randolph Hearst Jr.

Three divorces later, Cann joined the Royal Canadian Navy but broke his back in an explosion when his troopship was torpedoed by a Japanese submarine. After a brief recovery, he was loaned to the Netherlands government as a "war correspondent and cinematographer." On board HMAS *Australia* covering the October 1944 invasion of Leyte in the Philippines, Cann survived a Japanese dive-bomber attack that killed the ship's captain. By June 17, he decided to produce a documentary called *Shangri-La*.

And despite his unimpressive arrival to begin the film project, within a few days, Cann had persuaded Hastings, Captain Walter, and the others to recreate their arrival at the Shangri-La valley base camp from the crash site.

But now, Captain Walter at Camp Shangri-La and Colonel Elsmore at the Far East Command headquarters had to get them all back to Hollandia. After weighing several options, Elsmore focused on using gliders. He brought in Lieutenant Henry E. Palmer, an expert on light aircraft to assess the situation. After some reconnaissance, and despite some misgivings, Palmer "made a case for the high-altitude and downright strangest mission in the history of military gliders."

Prospects for the mission weren't particularly bright, since the planned operation was really a first-time experiment. The Army Air Corps had recently developed a method for retrieving gliders used in combat missions by picking the empty planes up with hooks and tow lines. And so Palmer suggested trying the snatch-and-tow method, but this time, with as many as five passengers inside and at a higher altitude than had ever before been attempted. Despite reservations, Elsmore announced the mission.

The first trial runs on a nearby island were plagued by injuries, ruined equipment, and growing doubts. Despite all this, plans for the mission continued. There really was no choice. For one reason, Hastings, Captain Walter, and the others were wearing out their welcome among the cannibals who surrounded their campsite; their presence in Shangri-La had interrupted the cycle of perpetual tribal wars. Consequently, Captain Walter had ordered everyone to stay in or near the camp as the days slowly went by.

While the operational kinks were being worked out at Wadke Island, a tiny speck about a hundred miles northwest of Hollandia, the rescuers in Shangri-La valley were preparing a makeshift landing area 400 yards long and 100 feet wide, outlined with red cargo parachutes and center-lined with white ones. They also constructed a device resembling two vaulting poles tied together with an inch-thick nylon cord, a sort of cradle to hold the glider towline.

In the proposed snatch, a C-47 would jerk the glider into the air, the glider would become fully airborne in sixty feet, and the two aircraft would fly on to safety, at least in theory. The fifteen members of Camp Shangri-La awoke on Thursday, June 28, to clear skies and a radio message announcing that this was the day.

Hastings, McCollum, Decker, and two paratroopers had only thirty minutes to gather their gear after the first glider dropped into the valley amidst thickening clouds. When it landed, they quickly jumped in, as Alex Cann aimed his camera at the scene for posterity. Some twenty or more natives helped them roll the glider into place for the launch.

Inside the glider, Lieutenant Palmer warned his passengers that the towline might break, prompting Hastings to grip her rosary even more tightly. She wondered out loud how the flimsy cabin would protect them if they crashed. The correct answer would have been "not much," but Palmer said nothing. And now they depended on Major William J. Samuels, piloting the C-47 transport plane *Leaking Louise* flying above them.

"Lower the boom," Samuels yelled at 9:47 that morning, seconds before a steel hook tied to *Leaking Louise* caught the loop tied to the glider, jerking plane and crew into the air, but not quickly enough to avoid another danger. They had snagged one of the white parachutes that marked the center of the runway and were dragging it; the glider was in real trouble.

After a few seconds, Major Samuels radioed Colonel Elsmore, then flying above him in a Flying Fortress, reporting that "I've pushed her as far as I can go." Elsmore quickly told Samuels he could forget about cutting the glider loose to save the C-47 engines. "Let them heat up, keep going." But now the passengers were listening to the parachute slapping against the fuselage. McCollum promptly fixed that, risking his life by pulling the chute in through the rear cargo door while holding on for dear life.

And with that, Hastings, McCollum, and Decker flew over the ruined remnants of the Gremlin scattered across the side of the mountain where it had all begun, watching *Leaking Louise* tow them toward freedom.

Chapter Thirteen

Operation Jericho

Many of the prisoners were sure this night was probably their last on earth. Amiens Prison had seen a great many judicial murders and much Gestapo torture and brutality, so except for those who were about to die, executions were routine. Most of those who died within these walls were simply patriots, members of the French Resistance movement, agents and ordinary people who helped their occupied country against the Germans and their own prostrate government at Vichy. They were held in a separate part of the prison, the "German side." The rest of the prison housed ordinary criminals.

Outside the grim stone walls, a bitter February night closed down like a shroud. Those about to die knew there could be no assistance, no miraculous delivery. Locked in their cells behind the thick stone walls, surrounded by a German garrison, in a city saturated with collaborationist police and officials, they were far from help. There could be no rescue mission from outside, for the Resistance had been badly shattered over the past months. Much of it was infested with informers, and those of its leaders not captured by the Gestapo or the French Milice (collaborationist French police) were on the run or in hiding.

This was 1944, the year of the Allied invasion, and much depended on information from within France: data on transportation, defenses, even the location of the Germans' V-1 buzz bombs reaching out toward London. Effective sabotage was crippled. Most of the heavy-duty transmitters sending information to London were in German hands. The damage to the Resistance apparatus must have crossed the minds of those about to die. Many were veterans, and among their fellow prisoners were at least one American and two Englishmen.

Worst of all, one of the French prisoners was the heart and soul of the Somme Resistance. If the Gestapo found out who he was and broke him, the entire network would crumble, and with it crucial preinvasion intelligence and information on the German missiles. The Allied intelligence chiefs knew the danger, and frankly agreed that this man had to be gotten out . . . or killed.

The French underground fighters who remained free were well aware of the plight of their comrades inside the prison. They had even weighed the possibility of an armed ground assault on the prison walls. They were a motley collection of shopkeepers, doctors, housewives, thieves, whores, and at least one pimp, but they shared a fierce patriotism. They would get their chance to help their imprisoned friends, but not in the way they imagined.

As time ran out, the underground tried to stay in existence and the Amiens prisoners thought grimly about what awaited them, thought of family, prayed, and prepared themselves as best they could. Meanwhile, in England, a remarkable man and an equally remarkable collection of planners, pilots, and navigators were preparing an astonishing feat of arms, no less than an aerial jailbreak, courtesy of the Royal Air Force.

The RAF outfit laid on for the task was comprised of 140 Wing, Squadrons Number 487; New Zealand, Number 464, Australian; and Number 21, British. From their airbase at Hunsdon, near London, the wing was flying "no ball" raids, strikes against German V-1 missile launching sites across the channel. These were experienced, highly professional airmen, many of the aircrew veterans of literally hundreds of missions into the hostile skies across the channel.

They were very good indeed. In fact, all three squadrons would be part of other daring strikes, including the March 1945 rooftop attack on the six-story Shell Building, Gestapo headquarters in Copenhagen. They left the building afire and were gone, covered by Mustangs, by the time the Germans could start to recover. A single plane was lost at zero altitude when it struck a building, but the Danish underground reported 151 Gestapo killed and some thirty Danes escaped.

The same squadrons also hit the Gestapo headquarters in Aarhus, Denmark, in October 1944. This raid, like the others, was truly an Allied affair. The aircrew were British, Canadians, Australians, and New Zealanders, and the covering Mustangs came from a Polish squadron. The target was not only the Germans in the building but especially the mass of carefully collected dossiers on thousands of Danes.

In spite of bad weather, that raid went perfectly. Delighted Danes waved the V-for-victory sign at the raiders, and on the run into the target a farmer ploughing his ground came to attention and saluted as the Mosquitos roared in toward the city and skimmed over the buildings as low as ten feet. The raiders struck their target hard, avoiding two nearby hospitals.

The raid was carried out without losses, except for a dented engine nacelle and one raider's tail wheel, left on an Aarhus building when the pilot closed in to return fire from a building window. One pilot had the memorable experience of watching one of a comrade's bombs hit its target, come out through the building's roof, and arch gracefully over his own aircraft.

The whole operation against the Amiens Prison—aptly called Jericho—had been prepared in haste and the deepest secrecy. Until a scale model of the Amiens Prison was unveiled on a table in the briefing room, none of the crews had any idea they were scheduled for the most audacious raid of the war, rivaled only by the Doolittle strike at Tokyo. Matter of factly, their leader, Air Vice Marshal Basil Embry, told the aircrews that they were on their way to blow holes in prison walls deep in France so that prisoners inside could run to safety. In daylight. In the middle of the day.

The whole idea might have seemed fantastic coming from about anybody but Embry, but he wore his credentials on his chest. He was a veteran of many missions into harm's way. He was once captured but couldn't be held for long. He simply killed his German guards and ran for it, escaping over the Pyrenees. The Germans put a 70,000-mark bounty on him, dead or alive, so he flew later missions as "Wing Commander Smith," even wearing a dogtag bearing his alias.

Embry was a stern taskmaster but a fine leader, intensely concerned with his men. When an assemblage of high-ranking officers pressed him to take the Vultee Vengeance for use in combat, Embry had been adamant: "I will not be a party to my men being killed in the Vultee Vengeance." And that was that.

The RAF would have to attack the prison soon, Embry said, since some of the prisoners were slated to be executed in the near future, probably on February 19. The group would be braving miserable weather, German flak, and a cloud of fighters, including the Focke-Wulf 190s of the Abbeville Boys. These were the pilots who painted the noses of their fighters yellow and followed the legendary Adolf Galland, the ace of aces of the war. They were a formidable lot.

So was the man who would command the wing during the raid. Embry had been forbidden to lead, a bitter disappointment, but he had confidence in the man who flew in his place. Percy Pickard—"Pick" to his pilots—was the wing commander, and himself a storied veteran of innumerable missions into the teeth of the Luftwaffe. Pickard had been an army officer of the King's African Rifles before the war but had been commissioned in the Royal Air Force in 1937. As it turned out, he and the RAF were made for each other.

He had been actively flying operational missions since 1940, including over a hundred nocturnal flights into occupied France, landing little Lysander liaison aircraft and Hudson bombers in pastures to deliver agents and supplies.

He was decorated for one astonishing mission: orbiting a pasture near Tournai at night in heavy fog for two hours. He finally was able to land and pick up his passengers . . . only to find his aircraft deeply bogged in muddy ground. For two more hours the Resistance—people from a nearby village, farm horses, even the local gendarme—labored to free the aircraft; not long before daylight, Pickard mushed through the pasture and took off just ahead of the Germans.

In 1942 he led the bombers that dropped paratroops, the lads who raided the German radar station at Bruneval, shot up the German garrison, took the radar apart, and made off by sea, taking a vital part of the set back to England. He also flew conventional missions; shot down on a bombing mission in the Ruhr, Pickard crash-landed in the North Sea, where he and his crew bobbed around in a rubber boat—in a mine field—until their little craft drifted clear and they could be rescued. Twice his Mosquito had been hit on low-level missions, but each time he and his observer made it home.

Pickard stood over six feet four, but he was nevertheless a gentle man who loved his wife and son, and cherished animals of all kinds from rabbits to snakes, and particularly his English sheepdog, Ming. He loved merrymaking, and his New Years' parties had a luminous reputation. During one of them, he was notable for breaking a wrist, falling from a roof beam along which he was walking.

Dead serious about their job, professional to their bootheels, the men of the wing nevertheless had a light side like their boss, very much in the RAF tradition. Visited by the king and queen at an airdrome at which the wing was earlier stationed, the flattered Pickard was asked by the king about the significance of a track of black barefoot prints leading up the mess wall and across the ceiling.

Pickard, realizing that appropriate wall- and ceiling-cleaning had been overlooked during the furious preparation for the royal visit, had to admit that the tracks were his. He had been hoisted up by his young pilots during an especially jovial party after the highly successful Bruneval raid, his feet covered with shoe polish. "But what," asked His Majesty, "are those two especially large blobs in the center of the ceiling?"

"I regret to say, sir," said Pickard, "that those are the marks of my bottom." He apologized, but he and his pilots found that royal couple had a sense of humor.

All three squadrons of the wing flew the DeHavilland Mosquito, probably the finest fighter-bomber of the war. The "wooden wonder," as she was called, was constructed largely of plywood from Canada and balsa wood from Ecuador. Her parts were put together in woodworking shops all across Britain—"every piano factory," Goering grumbled, when the Mosquito proved faster than any German fighter of the day. Then the final assembly took place at De Havilland, where the sections were put together in concrete molds, the glue bombarded with microwaves to hurry the drying.

Even the early prototype reached a speed of 392 miles per hours, an unheard-of speed for the day. The Mosquito's power came from a pair of Rolls-Royce Merlins, the same engine that drove the Spitfire, and made an ordinary airplane called the Mustang into a long-range wonder, the finest single-engine fighter of the war.

The Mosquito appeared in all sorts of configurations besides light bomber: She flew as a photo-reconnaissance aircraft, radar-equipped night-fighter, heavy-bomber escort, and one version, armed with rockets and a 57-millimeter cannon, was developed to stalk German U-boats. During the war, the fleet, agile aircraft flew more than 28,000 missions, one plane flying 213 sorties.

Mosquitos struck Berlin in early 1943, giving the lie to Goering's boast that no British bomber would ever reach the capital of Nazi Germany. "If the British bomb Berlin," he had boasted, "my name is Meir." Both Berliners and the men of the Luftwaffe have a sense of humor, and the fat field marshal was well known in both circles thereafter as "Herr Meir."

The Mosquito carried a prodigious sting. The airplanes that would attack the prison were armed with four machine guns and four cannon in addition to their bomb loads. Much thought had gone into those loads, and especially into how the bombs were to be dropped. Since the idea was to blow holes in the walls through which the prisoners could run to escape, and the RAF was coming in on the deck—"naught feet," as the pilots put it—the Mosquitos were in effect skip-bombing and using delayed-action ordnance at that.

They had to hold a speed well below what the airplane would do, and use great care to leave space between waves, so that the delayed-action bombs of one wave would not go off before the next wave flew clear. In addition to knocking down pieces of wall, the impact generated by the bombs would also, the planners hoped, shake open the locks on cell doors or spring their hinges.

One thing favored the attackers besides their daring, their experience, and the quality of their aircraft: The ground around the prison was relatively flat and free of trees, houses, or other obstructions, making low-level attack possible. They would arrive in waves of six airplanes on a front of about 100 yards. Each aircraft would drop its load of four bombs at once. If one wave failed to demolish its target, the next wave would follow up and bomb it.

Embry, Pickard, and their crews knew there was a substantial chance of civilian casualties inside the prison, but there was no help for that if the escape was to succeed. The French underground leadership knew it too, but was ready to help. The Resistance members, alerted to the possibility of the raid in the week before February 18, knew only that it would be around midday.

And so they collected bicycles, men, and vehicles near the prison around noon each day, ready to hide escapers and spirit them away. They included a stock of weapons as well, in case they had to rush gaps in the walls to help prisoners out to freedom. There was also a vast stock of identity documents, stolen or expertly forged, many with real seals.

The motor vehicles were powered by Gazogenes, which ran grumpily on gas from a wood-burning contraption perched on the rear. The Gazogene then pumped the gas into a peculiar-looking tank perched on the roof. They were ungraceful and ran at a glacial pace, but they were all that was available to the French civilian population—at least they would not attract unwanted attention from either the Germans or the puppet Vichy police.

The 17th of February was an impossible flying day. A solemn conference weighed the situation at Mongewell Park, Embry's headquarters. Then the 18th dawned cold and thickly overcast, miserable weather into which no civilian aircraft would ever have ventured. Snowstorms swept over parts of southern England and over the channel.

Nevertheless, the raid was a go, driven by the ominous knowledge that more delay, even a day, might be the death of more prisoners at Amiens. One frightening piece of information passed to the Resistance indicated that the execution would in fact be on the 19th, and a mass grave had already been dug.

The wing's attack was minutely orchestrated. The first squadron, 487 New Zealand, would split into two three-plane sections, each section to strike a different side of the walls. The Australians, also flying in two three-plane sections, would follow, attacking the corners of the main building. Six aircraft of 21 British were in reserve, ready to hit anything that wasn't destroyed or that Pickard ordered. Pickard would orbit over the prison, identifying targets that needed more work, and a photo-recon Mosquito would record the damage.

Each squadron would be covered by a squadron of burly Hawker Typhoon fighters. The big Typhoon, lineal descendant of the famous Hurricane, was designed as an interceptor. The "Tiffy," in RAF slang, had won its spurs as a fighter-bomber, fast, armed to the teeth, destroying more than 130 German tanks during the Normandy breakout at Avranches. It was also a first-class low-level fighter, a match for the Luftwaffe's Focke-Wulf 190 at the altitudes at which the Mosquitos would operate.

Pickard would watch for prisoners running through breaches in the walls, a sure sign of success. But if, he said, there were no escapers to be seen, 21 Squadron would be ordered in to bomb the jail itself. "We have been informed," he said, "that the prisoners would rather be killed by our bombs than by German bullets." It was something nobody wanted to do, but 21 Squadron was grimly prepared to strike the heart of the prison.

There would be, Pickard added, complete radio silence, and anybody who brought a bomb back to England would answer to him personally. And when someone asked about the precise course, the answer was vintage Pickard: "Bugger the course. Just follow me—you'll be all right."

The three squadrons took off into the murk of a miserable morning. It was still snowing over southeastern England, but meteorology held out hope that the weather would improve once they reached France. At the start, it couldn't have been worse. The snow poured in against the Mosquitos' canopies, clouds were down to a hundred feet or so, and there was no hope of keeping formation.

Several aircraft lost all touch with the others, including Pickard himself, and two Mosquitos narrowly avoided collision. Four crews were hopelessly lost, and at last had to turn back—they could not reach the prison in time to meet the exacting timetable of the raid. Three escort Typhoons also had to turn back—they also would have been too late over the target.

Still another pilot lost an engine over France. Flying too slow to press on, he jettisoned his bombs and turned for home. Hit by flak on the way, with only one arm and one leg working, blood streaming from his neck, he hung on grimly. His observer managed to give him a shot of morphine, and he flew for home. Miraculously, he would make it. The rest pressed on, flying so low that their propwash kicked up great clouds of snow, skimming so near rows of power poles and lines of poplars that some of the Mosquitos had to raise one wing to avoid collision.

But at the prison, the weather was better, and the attack went in as planned just as town churchbells tolled noon. The raiders fired on an astonished German patrol on the way in, and the aircraft dropped their bombs at zero altitude with remarkable accuracy, skimming over the prison walls as they climbed after their drop. The RAF film unit ground away, taking the same chances the bombers did, making repeated runs to continue filming.

As great breaches appeared in the walls, little figures began to run for open country, sprinting for their freedom through the gaps. They slipped and slithered in the ice and snow, but they kept going, some prisoners helping others either hurt or otherwise unable to run.

You could tell them from the Germans, said one RAF man, because every time a bomb went off, the Germans would dive to the ground, "but the prisoners [would] keep on running like hell." The bombs blew several small breaches in the north wall of the prison, a big one in the south wall, and an enormous hole where the west and north walls came together.

One aircraft dropped its load against the guardhouse and wall and climbed hard, skimming over a sort of gargoyle figure on the wall. Climbing away, the crew watched one bomb blow in the guardhouse, while two more tore into the wall. Some of the guard force lay dead or wounded in their mess hall; others wandered aimlessly through the ruins. Meanwhile, two prisoners—one a professional thief who picked the locks on the filing cabinets— were busily burning prisoner dossiers in the commandant's office. Two more—one a professional burglar—paused in their flight long enough to burgle the Gestapo headquarters, knife a guard, crack the safe, and burn more heaps of files.

The great escape went on, prisoners by the hundreds running to nearby streets where they walked innocently away, piled into the Gazogene fleet, or jumped on bicycles . . . and vanished. Some—as many as a hundred—changed clothes in commercial vans thoughtfully parked for the purpose. Prisoners helped each other without distinction as to which side of the prison they came from. There were no criminals running from the building, no political prisoners, only Frenchmen. Some stripped guards' bodies of their uniforms, becoming instant Germans. One, equipped with a white cane, tapped his way to freedom as a blind man.

A team of nine Resistance members, including at least one prostitute, raided several stores, led by a professional thief called Violette Lambert—at least, that was one of her names. Many of her team were also professional criminals, the women with bags carried under their clothing to receive their loot. The men carried overcoats over their arms, the sleeves sewed closed to carry their booty.

The stolen attire was meant to clothe the escapers, and the team of thieves stole so many articles that some had to return to their cars to unload and return for more. At last Violette saw one of her team being closely observed and shouted, "My bag's been stolen!" The man slipped away in the confusion.

Other prisoners, not so lucky or inventive, were recaptured, many of them wounded or injured. And a few chose not to escape. One doctor, unhurt and able to flee, chose to stay behind with the wounded prisoners and to help dig out wounded still trapped beneath the rubble of Amiens Prison. Other able-bodied prisoners stayed to help him.

Other escapers were quickly hidden: private homes, doctor's clinics, bordellos, any place to get the prisoners off the street quickly. Three were sheltered in a brothel and placed, the madam said, in a room between two rooms where she would send girls to entertain visitors from German military intelligence, "a tasty Amiens jail sandwich," she said. The madam was an original in any case: She seldom went anywhere without her grenades, one or two of which she left from time to time under German vehicles. "Financing escapes with money the Nazis spend here," she said, "is one of my greatest pleasures—the other is killing them."

Two other escapers seeking sanctuary—one a forger, the other a saboteur—were dressed in monk's habits, passed across

France from monastery to monastery in the company of real priests. More, concealed in the back of a horse-drawn van, survived when their driver was stopped by a member of the Milice, the French collaborationist police. "What's in the van?" asked the Vichy cop. "Some of the people who escaped from the prison," the driver answered; the Milice man took it as a bad joke and sent the van on its way.

Many escaped prisoners were hidden in the underground vaults of a private clinic run by the father-and-son doctors Poulain, the same vaults they had used as refuge for Jews hunted by the Nazis. The vaults were hard to find, for they were concealed below the first basement—the morgue. Other escapers were hidden in plain sight, put to bed with their faces bandaged, victims of a "road accident." Others became "expectant mothers," mounded with covers. "When are they due to deliver?" the Gestapo asked. "About three o'clock in the morning," the doctor said. "Why that time?" asked the German. "Nobody knows," said the doctor, "but that was when most babies traditionally decided to be born." The Germans bought it all. The bombing went so well that even the demanding Pickard was satisfied. The British 21 Squadron, standing by to bore in and finish the job, heard Pickard calling, "Red Daddy." It was the call to turn and go; their extra bombs would not be needed. And then the wing's aircraft were on their way home, roaring across France almost on the ground, chased by flak, pursued by Luftwaffe Messerschmidt 109s and Focke-Wulf 190s. The Typhoons fought off many of the German aircraft, and the Mosquitos fought back with their own formidable armament, shooting down several of the pursuing German fighters. Squadron leader Ian McRichie crash-landed in a snowy pasture, partially paralyzed, his observer dead. McRichie would survive, a wounded prisoner.

As the remaining raiders reached the channel, scattered and exhausted, the weather closed down again. Gray waves and thick snow showers cut visibility to almost zero. If they dived under the shelter of the clouds, visibility disappeared altogether. And then, as the Germans turned away about mid-channel, and the earth of England passed under the Mosquitos' bellies, Hunsdon radioed landing instructions, staggering the planes' altitudes to avoid collision between tired pilots and damaged aircraft.

Nobody had rested at Hunsdon or over at Embry's headquarters. Everyone wondered and prayed. They knew the raid had been a success, but nobody knew how many of the Mosquitos were coming home. Recon aircraft swept over Amiens and the homeward path of the raiders, looking for downed aircraft. Now Mosquitos were coming back, queuing up to land, but nobody knew what had happened to McRichie or Pickard.

But Dorothy Pickard knew. Ming, Pickard's beloved sheepdog, had collapsed, vomiting blood. A sort of supernatural bond existed between man and dog. Ming always fretted when Pickard flew, but she relaxed when her master was back on the ground, even before his wife knew Pick was back safely. She trusted Ming's instincts: "Pick's dead," his wife said. And it was so. Somehow his dog's sixth sense knew her master was gone for good.

For Pickard—good commander—had stayed too long over the target, assessing the damage to the prison walls and watching over his men as they flew clear. At last turned for home, he was bounced, as the RAF put it, by two Focke-Wulf 190s, diving from higher altitude to offset the greater speed of the Mosquito. Pickard made a fight of it, nailing one German fighter, which ran for home. But the cannon of the second Luftwaffe aircraft ripped the tail from Pick's aircraft and the plane smashed into the ground and burst into flame. There was very little left.

Local civilians rushed to help, using sticks to try to pull out the bodies of Pick and his longtime friend and navigator, Flight

Lieutenant Alan Bradley, but the flames were too hot and the Mosquito's remaining ammunition began to cook off from the heat. Only later could they recover the remains of the crew, and one of them cut Pickard's wings and ribbons from his uniform, hoping to hinder any identification by the Germans. In time, the girl who removed them sent them to his wife. Other villagers took and hid a camera they found in the aircraft and burned Bradley's maps on the theory that either one might somehow aid the Germans.

Pickard had been awarded a Distinguished Flying Cross and the Distinguished Service Order three times over an illustrious career. He was also awarded the Czech Military Medal for his leadership of a Czech squadron flying from England . . . and he was "Mentioned in Despatches," a uniquely British commendation. Some thought he should have been given the Victoria Cross for his leadership and sacrifice above Amiens.

Long after the raid, French citizens came to put flowers on the graves of Pickard and Bradley; they even went so far as to expunge the German grave markings and substitute their own.

He was gone now, mourned by his family, his beloved sheepdog, and hundreds of men who wore the horizon blue of the RAF—the world was much the poorer for his passing, but the success of the Amiens raid was his best memorial. The German guard force had suffered heavily, the commandant dead, and an estimated twenty killed and seventy wounded, even though the Germans publicly said they had no casualties at all. But even the Germans' own records admitted that more than 250 prisoners had gotten away and had not been recaptured. In fact, the total was substantially greater.

Eighty-seven had died in the bombing and received a mass funeral carefully orchestrated by the Vichy French authorities.

Predictably, the tame French press fulminated at the British, carefully parroting the party line that the raid was a crime. The funeral was a sad time, but even that had its bright side, for in the cortege of one of the dead, six wanted men walked piously away from the convent where they had been hidden.

Whatever the supine French press said, the French Resistance and most of the French people knew better. And fifteen weeks after the strike at Amiens, the Allies came ashore in Normandy.

CHAPTER FOURTEEN

Ming, the Dog Who Knew

PICK PICKARD'S RELATIONSHIP WITH MING, HIS ENGLISH sheepdog, is the stuff of legend. She had been a wedding present to Pickard's wife, Dorothy, but her deepest allegiance was to Pickard himself. And her uncanny, extraordinary sense of her master's situation kept her restless and apprehensive when Pickard flew. She somehow knew when Pickard took off, and trotted outside to watch and wait until she sensed his return from the mission.

Then in June 1940, returning from a night raid into the Ruhr, Pickard's damaged bomber crash-landed in the North Sea. And Ming knew. At 3:20 in the morning Ming pulled at Dorothy's blankets; assuming her dog wanted to go outside to do her business, Dorothy let Ming out—but the dog sat down and stared at the sky. When daylight came, Dorothy took Ming to the airfield, and the two waited for news of their man. And late in the afternoon, Ming suddenly went to sleep.

Pickard's wife called operations and was told that Pickard had crashed but was safe. He and all his crew had been fished out of their rubber boat . . . in a minefield. And when Pickard was back in England, his wife asked him if knew when the crash occurred. He did, he said, for his watch had broken from the impact of the crash . . . at 3:20.

On another mission into France to aid the Resistance, Pickard flew his unarmed plane back in daylight, having spent most of the night with a group of Frenchmen, digging his aircraft out of a boggy field, in constant danger from the German enemy. Dorothy knew from early morning that Pickard was in danger: Ming had again tugged at her blankets until Dorothy let her out. Ming sat down in the snow until about 5:30 a.m., about the time Pickard at last took off into the French night, headed for England.

Then Ming scratched at the door, found a spot in front of the fireplace, and went to sleep. She repeated her performance on another occasion, as Pickard nursed a damaged Mosquito back to England; when Pickard landed safely—at another airfield—the dog went back to bed.

On the day of the Amiens raid, Ming braved the bitter cold and sat outside as usual, watching the stormy sky. And then, about the time her master smashed into the French earth and died, Ming collapsed, and would not respond even to Dorothy Pickard. She knew her master was gone, and so did his wife.

After the war, Dorothy Pickard moved to Rhodesia, and Ming went with her. And there, in 1952, Pickard's widow was awakened at night by whimpering from Ming, who had been very ill. She got up to let the dog out, and as she did so, she thought she heard four whistles, the signal with which Pickard had called Ming to walk or chase rabbits, her favorite pastime. Dorothy Pickard looked around her garden but found nobody. And when she went back inside, she found Ming sitting up, her head moving as it had when she waited for Pickard to return to England all those years before. Then Dorothy heard the whistles again; Ming looked up and collapsed, dead.

It was the night of the 18th of February, eight years to the day after her master had died.

CHAPTER FIFTEEN

Fighting Man

IT IS NOT RECORDED WHAT THE GERMAN COMMANDER SAID when he learned that one of his men had been spitted by a broadhead arrow.

It was May 1940, and the German officer's unit was attacking toward a village called l'Epinette, near Bethune, France. Five of his soldiers took cover behind a farmyard wall, sheltered from the fire of British rear guards covering the retreat of the British Expeditionary Force to the channel. Without warning, one German crumpled, the feathered tip of an arrow sticking out of his chest. From a small farm building on their flank, rifle fire tore into the others.

Although he might have known that his enemies were soldiers of the Manchester Regiment, the German leader could not have known that they were led by the formidable Captain Jack Churchill. It was Churchill's arrow that skewered the luckless German, while his men's rifles accounted for the rest. The Manchesters were formidable soldiers and always had been, precisely the sort of men Jack Churchill was cut out to lead. Still, however deadly, a war bow and arrows were surely anachronisms in modern war. But then, so was the bowman.

John Malcolm Thorpe Fleming Churchill was a professional soldier, scion of an old Oxfordshire family. Born in Hong Kong, Churchill had graduated from Sandhurst in 1926 and was commissioned in the Manchesters, a storied regiment with battle honors dating back to the eighteenth century. The regiment had been raised as the 63rd and 96th Regiments of Foot, and had shed their blood for Britain all across the world. Forty-two battalions of Manchesters served in World War I alone.

His younger brother Tom also became a Manchesters officer, and in time would rise to major general, retiring in 1962. His younger brother, called Buster, opted for the Royal Navy's Fleet Air arm, and died for his country off Malta during the fierce fighting of Operation Pedestal.

That Jack Churchill was a free spirit was obvious from the beginning of his service, even in an army rich in such men. For example, while serving in Burma before the outbreak of World War II, he attended a course in signals at Poona, in India. It might appear odd to some that Churchill took his motorcycle all the way from Rangoon to Poona, but did not seem at all remarkable, at least to Churchill, to return the 1,500 miles from Poona to Calcutta—from whence he was to take ship for Rangoon—riding his bike. Along the way he was delayed by a large and hostile water buffalo, but returned to his unit in time to serve in the Burma Rebellion of 1930–1932.

Unusual hazards and difficulties never meant much to Churchill. On the same motorcycle, he had traveled the 500 miles through Burma from Maymyo to Rangoon, a trip substantially complicated by an absence of roads. He therefore followed the railroad line, crossing the dozens of watercourses by pushing the bike along a rail while he walked on the cross-ties. Everything in life was a challenge to him. Among them was mastering the bagpipes, a peculiar attachment for an Englishman. His love affair with the pipes seems to have originated in Maymyo, where he studied under the pipe major of the Cameron Highlanders.

Back in England in 1932, Churchill kept on studying the pipes, but the peacetime army had begun to pall. Jack Churchill was one of those unusual men designed to lead others in combat, and such men are often restless in time of peace.

And perhaps, as his biographer commented,

> *certain eccentricities—brought on no doubt through frustration—such as piping the orderly officer to the Guard Room at three o'clock of a morning, and studying the wrong pre-set campaign in preparation for his promotion exam, precluded any chance of promotion for the time being and made the break, after a chat with his commanding officer, inevitable.*

When Churchill managed to get himself reprimanded for using a hot water bottle, a distinctly nonmilitary piece of equipment—he circumvented this nicety of military protocol by substituting a piece of rubber tubing, which he filled from the nearest hot-water tap. And then there was the day on which he appeared on parade carrying an umbrella, a mortal sin in any army. When asked by the battalion adjutant what he meant by such outlandish behavior, Churchill replied, "Because it's raining, sir," an answer, however accurate, not calculated to endear him to the frozen soul of any battalion adjutant.

Whatever the reason, after ten years of service, Churchill resigned his commission and turned to commercial ventures. A job on the editorial staff of a Nairobi paper did not please him, and so he turned to other tasks. Among other things, he worked as model in magazine ads and as a movie extra. He appeared in *The Drum*, a movie of fighting on the Northwest Frontier in which he could play the bagpipes. And because he had rowed on the River Isis, he won a cameo in *A Yank at Oxford,* in which he pulled the bow oar in the Oxford shell, with movie star Robert Taylor at stroke.

He continued his piping at the same time, and in the summer of 1938 placed second in the officers' class of the piping championships at Aldershot. It was an extraordinary feat, since he was the only Englishman among the seventy or so competitors. During these years out of harness, Churchill practiced another skill as well—archery—which he had first tried after returning to Britain from Burma. His expertise with the bow got him work in *Sabu* and *The Thief of Baghdad.* And with typical Churchillian determination, he became so good with the bow that he shot for Britain at the World Championships in Oslo in 1939.

By then, however, the long ugly shadows of war were stretching across Europe. As the German army smashed into Poland, Churchill returned to the army and the Manchester Regiment, and was shipped off to France. "I was," he said later, "back in my red coat; the country having got into a jam in my absence." He was obviously happy to be soldiering again.

Patrolling a quiet stretch of France during the pre-blitz "*sitzkrieg*" of late 1939 and early 1940 did not suit a man of Churchill's warlike temperament. And so, along with a bevy of other free spirits, he volunteered for the force assembling to go and help the Finnish army, then under attack by the Red Army. That expedition was canceled before it could leave for Finland, and Churchill returned to the Manchesters in time to meet the German juggernaut as it crashed into Holland, Belgium, and France in May of 1940. By that time, Churchill was second in command of an infantry company in the regiment's Second Battalion.

During the British Expeditionary Force's fighting retreat, Churchill remained aggressive, unwilling to give up a yard of ground without extracting the maximum cost from the enemy.

He was especially fond of raids and counterattacks, leading small groups of picked soldiers against the advancing Germans. He presented an eccentric, almost medieval figure at the head of his men, carrying not only his war bow and arrows, but his sword as well.

As befitted his love of things Scottish, Churchill carried the basket-hilted claymore (technically a *claybeg*, the true claymore being an enormous two-handed sword). Later on, asked by a general who awarded him a decoration why he carried a sword in action, Churchill is said to have answered, "In my opinion, sir, any officer who goes into action without his sword is improperly dressed."

The war diary of Fourth Infantry Brigade, to which Churchill's battalion belonged, commented on this extraordinary figure, "One of the most reassuring sights of the embarkation [from Dunkirk] was the sight of Captain Churchill passing down the beach with his bows and arrows. His high example and his great work were a great help to the 4th Infantry Brigade."

During the retreat, Churchill took command of his company when his company commander was wounded, and it was during this fighting that he spitted his hapless German soldier with, as the chronicles of Henry V's wars would put it, "a cloth-yard shaft." One of his brother officers—an old friend—saw him about that time, chugging across the Flanders plain on a small motorcycle, his bow tied to the frame, arrows sticking out of one of the panniers on the back, a German officer's cap hanging on the headlight. "Ah!" said Churchill, spotting his friend, "Hullo, Clark! Got anything to drink?"

Once Churchill had dismounted, his friend noticed dried blood smeared across one ear and asked Churchill about the injury. German machine gun, said Churchill casually. His men had shouted at him to run but, he said, he was simply too tired.

He won his first Military Cross during the retreat to the channel, when he hitched six trucks together to salvage a disabled British tank; although in the end he could not save the tank, he did rescue a wounded British officer.

His close call did not seem to impress Churchill in the least—then and afterward, he seemed to be one of those extraordinary men who thrive on danger and fear it not at all. Some fellow soldiers are said to have called him "Mad Jack," and the nickname was not altogether undeserved.

Churchill made it to Dunkirk—allegedly by bicycle, his bow and arrows hanging from the frame. From that terrible beach he was lifted back to England—so was his Manchester friend—courtesy of the gallantry of the Royal Navy and a horde of courageous civilian boats and ships, and it was there he heard of a new outfit being formed. It sounded like precisely the sort of unit Churchill was cut out for. Requests for volunteers for this new duty were somewhat vague, but they promised aggressive service at least, and that was good enough for Churchill. Whatever a Commando was, he would be one.

His training in Scotland produced an unexpected dividend for Churchill. There he met Rosamund Denny, the daughter of a Scottish shipbuilding baronet. They were married in Dumbarton in the spring of 1941, a union that would produce two children and last until Churchill's death fifty-five years later.

Churchill took to Commando operations like a duck to water—including the icy water of Scottish lochs. He was at home on the steep hills, in the rain and the mud. He lived and breathed training, leading, driving, setting the example, praising excellence, and damning sloth and carelessness. His ad hoc lectures to his soldiers were couched in the plain language his men understood and liked, for instance:

There's nothing worse than sitting on your bum bottom doing nothing just because the enemy happens to leave you alone for a moment while he has a go at the unit on your flank . . . support your neighbor any way you can.

There was also a bit of a downside to Jack Churchill. On those happy occasions when the Commandos were not in the field at night, he was sometimes given to awakening everybody in the billet hotel at Largs, Scotland, shattering the night with pipe music. No piper could possibly understand why some of the world would rather sleep than listen to martial piping, however expert, and he was no exception. His comrades could only grit their teeth and hope that he would soon tire or think of something quieter to do.

The Commandos' eternal training ended on December 27, 1941, with the brilliantly successful assault on the German garrison at Vaagso, the Norwegian town on Nord Fjord. Churchill commanded two companies in the attack, charged with taking out the German shore batteries on Maaloy Island, which lay in the icy fjord opposite Vaagso town. In vintage Churchill fashion, he stood in the lead landing craft as it forged in toward the shore, his pipes screaming "The March of the Cameron Men."

He then waded ashore at the head of his men, sword in hand, and charged ahead, as one account put it, "into the thick smoke, uttering warlike cries." Maaloy and its battery fell quickly. Churchill and his men killed or took prisoner the garrison, including two women who, as one account of the raid genteelly put it, "might be described as camp followers." While heavy fighting continued for a while in Vaagso itself, the landing force would not be troubled by the cannon of Maaloy. Churchill's signal to the raid commander was terse: "Maaloy battery and island captured. Casualties slight. Demolitions in progress. Churchill."

The Commandos had stung the Germans badly; in time, the Norwegian garrisons would be heavily reinforced with troops critically required elsewhere. The German garrison at Vaagso had ceased to exist; the raiders took back with them some hundred prisoners and about seventy volunteers for the free Norwegian forces. The expedition had also sunk about 15,000 tons of shipping and destroyed not only docks and warehouses but also the vital fish-oil plants so important to German ammunition production and to dietary supplements for the German armed forces. And German troops near any coastline would not sleep quite as well as they had before Vaagso.

As the raiders prepared to leave Vaagso and Maaloy, a British demolition charge exploded so close to Churchill that it "blew him up," in the words of one account. Another story says that a demolitions man "thoughtlessly blew down a wall he happened to be leaning against." Still another version—which sounds eminently Churchillian—relates he was celebrating the raid's success with a bit of liberated Moselle wine when the charge went off, and a chunk of broken bottle slashed into Churchill's forehead.

Whatever happened, Churchill had another wound—or at least a sort of wound—to show for his successful leadership at Maaloy. As he himself joked later, "I had to touch it up from time to time with Rosamund's lipstick to keep the wounded hero story going." He also had his second Military Cross.

In the autumn of 1943, Churchill won the Distinguished Service Order for an astonishing exploit during the Salerno landings. Ashore in command of No. 2 Commando—also present were some other Churchills, such as his brother Tom and Captain Randolph, son of the prime minister—Churchill led his men in heavy and confused fighting around the town of Marina. Their mission was to destroy German ability to place artillery fire on the western half of the Bay of Salerno. Churchill directed the final counterattack, which broke the last German attempt to destroy the Commando beachhead.

During the ferocious Salerno fighting, No. 2 Commando found itself fighting as line infantry—as did its American counterparts, the Rangers—a role for which neither Commandos nor Rangers were designed. Casualties were heavy, but the Commandos beat back every German attack. For Churchill, the high point of the fighting was the night attack on a town called Piegoletti (sometimes Piegolelli). He organized his men into six parallel columns and, since the heavy undergrowth ruled out any chance of a silent advance, sent them charging through the darkness shouting, "Commando!"

The yelling not only minimized the risk of Commandos shooting each other in the gloom but also confused the German defenders, to whom this fierce shouting seemed to come from all directions in the blackness of the night. The attack carried all its objectives and bagged 136 prisoners.

Churchill himself was far in front of his troopers. Sword in hand, accompanied only by a corporal named Ruffell, he advanced into the town itself. Undiscovered by the enemy, he and Ruffell heard German soldiers digging in all around them in the gloom. The glow of a cigarette in the darkness told them the location of a German sentry post. What followed, even Churchill later admitted, was "a bit Errol Flynn-ish."

The first German sentry post, manned by two soldiers, was taken in silence. Churchill, his sword blade gleaming in the night, appeared like a demon from the darkness, ordered *"Haende hoch!"* and got results. He gave one German prisoner to Ruffell, then slipped his revolver lanyard around the second sentry's neck and led him off to make the rounds of the other guards. Each post, lulled into a sense of security by the voice of their captive comrade, surrendered to this fearsome apparition with the ferocious mustache and the naked sword.

Altogether, Churchill and Corporal Ruffell collected forty-two prisoners, complete with their personal weapons and a mortar they were manning in the village. Churchill and his claymore took the surrender of ten men in a bunch around the mortar. He and his NCO then marched the whole lot back into the British lines. As Churchill himself described the event, it all sounded rather routine:

> *I always bring my prisoners back with their weapons; it weighs them down. I just took their rifle bolts out and put them in a sack, which one of the prisoners carried. [They] also carried the mortar and all the bombs they could carry and also pulled a farm cart with five wounded in it. . . . I maintain that, as long as you tell a German loudly and clearly what to do, if you are senior to him he will cry "Jawohl" and get on with it enthusiastically and efficiently whatever the . . . situation. That's why they make such marvelous soldiers.*

Churchill's next assignment took him to the Adriatic, where British units and Tito's Yugoslav partisan forces struck at the German garrisons along the Dalmatian coast. In January of 1944, Churchill—leading No. 2 Commando, about a thousand Yugoslav partisans, and some antiaircraft and machine gun attachments—became commandant of the island of Vis, the last Dalmation Island not in German hands.

From Vis, the campaign against the German-held Adriatic islands was carried on at sea by the RAF and by small boats of the Royal Navy. Ever ready for raids and excursions, Churchill sent some of his Commandos along with the navy as boarding party, to swarm over the side of any ship carrying supplies to the enemy.

Small groups of Commandos also landed by night to harass the German garrisons on other Dalmatian islands. The commander of one such party, Lieutenant B. J. Barton, discovered that the German commandant on the island of Brac was much given to mistreatment of the island population. Barton, disguised as a Yugoslav shepherd, hid his Sten gun in pieces inside a load of wood on a donkey, slipped into the German headquarters village, killed the commandant, and got away clean.

A series of successful raids by Commandos and partisans hurt the Germans, and in May of 1944 a more ambitious attack by British and Yugoslav crews was planned on the German-held Yugoslav island of Brac—and it was here that Jack Churchill's amazing luck at last ran out. The operation required attacks on three separate hilltop positions, each of them dug in, mutually supporting, protected by wire and mines, and covered by artillery. Several Allied forces would have to work in cooperation; one of these, a reinforced Commando unit plus a large contingent of partisans, Jack Churchill would lead himself.

While partisan attacks on the main German position got nowhere, 43 (Royal Marine) Commando went in to the attack on the vital hill called Point 622. Pushing ahead in clear moonlight through wire and minefields, 43 Commando carried the hilltop but was forced to fall back with heavy casualties. Churchill now sent 40 Commandos—also Royal Marines—in against the hill and led them himself, playing the bagpipes. The leading troop went in yelling, shooting from the hip, and overran the German positions on 622.

But between casualties on the way up the hill and more casualties from very heavy German fire on the top, Churchill quickly found himself isolated with only a handful of defenders around him. There were only six Commandos on the hilltop, and three of those were wounded, two of them very badly. "I was distressed," said Churchill with memorable understatement, "to find that everyone was armed with revolvers except myself, who had an American carbine."

Still the little party fought on, until the revolver ammunition was gone and Churchill was down to a single magazine for his carbine. A German mortar round killed three of his little party and wounded still another, leaving Churchill as the only unwounded defender on the hilltop. It was the end. Churchill turned to his pipes, playing "Will ye no come back again?" until German grenades burst in his position and he was stunned by a fragment from one of them. He regained consciousness to discover German soldiers "prodding us, apparently to discover who was alive."

Long after the end of the war, Churchill was pleased to hear that the German account of the fighting for the hill described his lonely piping as "the doleful sound of an unknown musical instrument."

Churchill would play his pipes one more time—at the funeral of fourteen Commandos who died on the slopes of Hill 622. He and his surviving men escaped killing by the Gestapo under Hitler's foul "Commando order" through the chivalry of one Captain Thuener of the Wehrmacht. "You are a soldier, as I am," the captain told Churchill. "I refuse to allow these civilian butchers to deal with you. I shall say nothing of having received this order." After the war, Churchill was able to personally thank Thuener for his decency and to help him stay out of the merciless hands of the Russians.

Churchill was flown to Sarajevo and then on to Berlin, there apparently being some notion that he was a relative of Winston Churchill. There is also a story that on leaving the aircraft, he left behind a burning match or candle in a pile of paper, producing a fire and considerable confusion. During the inquiry that followed, Churchill innocently told a furious Luftwaffe officer that the army officer escorting Churchill had been smoking and reading the paper on board the aircraft.

Churchill spent some time in solitary confinement, and in time he ended up in Sachsenhausen concentration camp. That infamous prison was only one more challenge to Churchill. In September of 1944, he and an RAF officer crawled under the wire through an abandoned drain and set out to walk to the Baltic coast. Their luck was not in, however, and they were recaptured near the coastal city of Rostock, only a few miles from the sea. In time, they were moved to a camp at Niederdorf, in Austria.

Here, Churchill watched for another opportunity to escape, keeping a small rusty can and some onions hidden in his jacket in case a sudden opportunity should present itself. And on an April night in 1945, it did. The chance came when the camp's lighting system failed.

Churchill seized the moment and walked away from a work detail, disappearing into the darkness and heading for the Alps and the Italian frontier. Liberating vegetables from Austrian gardens and cooking them in his tin can, he walked steadily south. Keeping off the roads, he crossed the Brenner Pass into Italy and headed for Verona, some 150 miles away.

And on the eighth day of his escape, hobbling along on a sprained ankle, Churchill caught sight of a column of armored vehicles, their hulls carrying the unmistakable white star of the United States Army. He managed to flag down one vehicle and persuade the crew that in spite of his scruffy appearance he was indeed a British colonel. As he later told his old friend and biographer, Rex King-Clark, "I couldn't walk very well and was so out of breath I could scarcely talk, but I still managed a credible Sandhurst salute, which may have done the trick."

Churchill was free but frustrated. The European war was almost over and he had missed much of it, including the chance for further promotion and perhaps the opportunity to lead a Commando brigade. Nevertheless, hope sprang eternal. "However," he said to friends, "there are still the Nips, aren't there?"

There were. And so Churchill was off to Burma, where the largest land war against Japan was still raging. Here, too, however, he met frustration, for by the time he reached India, Hiroshima and Nagasaki had disappeared in mushroom clouds, and the war abruptly ended. For a warrior like Churchill, the end of the fighting was bittersweet. "You know," he said to a friend, only half joking, "if it hadn't been for those damned Yanks we could have kept the war going for another ten years."

The abrupt departure of Japan from the war was a distinct disappointment to Churchill, especially since he had risen to command of a Commando brigade in the Far East. Still, there were other brushfire wars still smoldering, and in November of 1945 he reported home from Hong Kong that "As the Nips have double-crossed me by packing up, I'm about to join the team v the Indonesians," who were by then casting covetous eyes on Sarawak, Borneo, and Brunei. British and Commonwealth troops killed or expelled the invaders, but Jack missed this little war as well.

By the next year he had transferred to the Seaforth Highlanders and was looking forward to jump school, where, at the age of forty, he qualified as a paratrooper. He took a little time off in 1946, this time for the movies. Twentieth-Century Fox was making *Ivanhoe* with Churchill's old rowing companion Robert Taylor and wanted him to appear as an archer, firing from the wall of Warwick Castle. Churchill took the assignment, flown off to the job in an aircraft provided by the movie company.

Churchill might have thought that he was through with war, but he was not. After World War II ended, after he qualified as a parachutist and transferred to the Seaforth Highlanders, he ended up in Palestine as second in command of First Battalion, the Highland Light Infantry (HLI). And it was there, in the spring of 1948, just before the end of the British mandate over that troubled land, that he again risked his life for other people.

Those were dangerous days, with much blood—Jewish, Arab, and British—shed by Arab terrorists and by Jewish radicals, notably the so-called Stern Gang. And on a day in May a Jewish medical convoy—ambulances, trucks, and buses—was ambushed by Arabs on a narrow street in Jerusalem, not far from a small HLI detachment at a place called Tony's Post. Churchill rushed to the site in a Dingo, a small armored car. This one had its turret removed for repair, but it gave him a semblance of protection at least.

Accurately assessing the potential for mass murder by the Arab terrorists, he radioed for two Staghounds, heavy cannon-armed armored cars, and these were diverted from convoy protection and dispatched to him. It would take time for the armored cars to reach him, however, and while they were on the way, Churchill acted. He drove down to the beleaguered convoy in a large armored personnel carrier, covered by the only escort available, an open-topped Bren gun carrier and a small police armored car armed with a machine gun. Leaving his tiny convoy, swinging a walking stick, he walked calmly into the open, down the road to the convoy.

Marching into the teeth of the battle around the convoy, he must have been quite a sight. Since he had just come from a battalion parade, he was resplendent in full dress uniform: kilt, glengarry bonnet, red-and-white diced stockings, Sam Browne belt, and white spats. And, as usual, he later made light of this extraordinary cold courage: "I grinned like mad from side to side," he said afterward,

> as people are less likely to shoot at you if you smile at them.
> . . . [My] outfit in the middle of the battle, together with my

*grinning at them, may have made the Arabs laugh because
most of them have a sense of humour. Anyway, they didn't
shoot me!*

Churchill spoke to the occupants of one bus and offered to
drive his big armored personnel carrier down to the convoy and
make as many trips as necessary to evacuate the patients and
their medical personnel. He warned those at the convoy that
there might be casualties when they moved to the British vehicle,
and one of the Jews asked whether he would not first drive off
the Arabs. He patiently explained that he could not; there were
hundreds of Arabs and he had only twelve men.

After a discussion with one of the doctors, as Churchill stood
in the open, his offer was refused. "Thank you very much but we
do not want your help. The Haganah [the Jewish defense force]
will save us." Churchill walked down the convoy repeating his
offer, but was uniformly refused. By now one of Churchill's men
had been mortally wounded, and he ran back to his vehicles and
sent them out of harm's way. Returning to Tony's Post, he covered
the Jewish convoy with small-arms fire until Arab gasoline bombs
and rifle fire destroyed the Jewish vehicles and most of their passengers. The Haganah had not arrived to save them after all, and
seventy-seven Jews died in the narrow street.

Later Churchill engineered the evacuation of some seven
hundred Jews—patients, staff, and students—from the university
and hospital atop Jerusalem's Mount Scopus. Churchill made an
early run up Scopus in his jeep, accompanied by Eli Davis, the
deputy medical director of the hospital. Here is how Davis later
told the story:

*Major Churchill told me there was a slight chance of getting
through . . . because the Arabs saw the British meant business.*

He agreed to make the trip up to Scopus and invited me along.
The Major took a Jeep and his driver. I sat, while he stood in
the Jeep twirling his stick. He looked as though he were on
parade in London.

Jack Churchill never changed, never lost his flair for the
unusual, not to say the flamboyant. In his later years, passengers
on a London commuter train were often startled when an older
male passenger would rise, open a window, and hurl his briefcase
out into the night. The passenger would then leave the car and
wait by the train's door until it stopped at the next station. It was
Churchill, of course, enjoying his little gesture and reasonably
sure that his fellow passengers could not know he had thrown
the case into the garden of his house. It also saved him carrying
it home from the station.

In later years, Churchill served as an instructor at the land-air
warfare school in Australia, where he became a passionate devotee of the surfboard. Back in England, he was the first man to
ride the Severn River's five-foot tidal bore and designed his own
board. He finally retired from the army—with two awards of the
Distinguished Service Order—in 1959. He went right on working, now as a Ministry of Defense civilian, overseeing the training
of Cadet Force youngsters in the London District.

One of his old friends wrote later that Churchill liked the job
not only because of his association with the enthusiastic Cadets
but also because the job gave him an office in Horse Guards at
Whitehall, and a window from which he could watch troopers
of the Household Cavalry mounting guard in a courtyard below
him. He was older now but still very much the warrior.

Churchill and his wife, Rosamund, could spend more time
together now, and they spent part of it sailing coal-fired steam
launches on the Thames between Oxford and Richmond,

Churchill decked out in an impeccable yachting cap and Rosa-mund giving appropriate sailing orders to her husband. Churchill was also well known for his intricate and accurate radio-controlled models of ships—mostly warships, of course—all so carefully engineered and built that they were much sought after by collectors.

Jack Churchill passed away peacefully at his home in Surrey in the spring of 1996, but he left a legacy of daring that survives to this day. One respected publication dealing with the Commandos features large color drawings of Commando uniforms, insignia, and weaponry. And one of the illustrations is of Mad Jack Churchill, complete with claymore.

Jack Churchill was one of that rare and happy breed for whom war is their element. That does not mean that he did not hate the suffering that war caused; it was simply that he thrived on the excitement and relished the chance to achieve and excel. His whole philosophy was pretty well summed up by a couplet he scribbled on a postcard he sent to a friend, a card whose face bore the regimental colors:

> No Prince or Lord has tomb so proud
> As he whose flag becomes his shroud.

He might have been describing himself.

CHAPTER SIXTEEN

Operation Halyard

HITLER'S WAR MACHINE RAN ON WHEAT, MEAT, AND OIL. Without any one of these, the blitzkrieg would grind to a halt. The homeland and the conquered lands could produce enough to feed the German armed forces; the problem was what to put in the fuel tanks of the armored vehicles and the transport, the fighters and the bombers, the trains and municipal heating plants—which was why so much depended on the Romanian oilfields of Ploesti, a nineteen-square-mile complex of wells, tank farms, and seven major refineries.

The complex lay in northern Romania, just across the heights of the Carpathian Mountains and some thirty-five miles from the capital of Bucharest. By 1942 Ploesti was turning out something in the neighborhood of a million tons of oil each month; its value to the German war effort was incalculable.

The Western Allies recognized the critical importance of the Ploesti installation; taking it out of operation would clearly advance the end of the war and save a great many lives. Trouble was, the Germans could see the importance of Ploesti as clearly as the Allies could; of all their conquests, in practical terms, this was one of the most precious jewels in the Nazi crown.

They protected it accordingly, surrounding it with an extensive network of massed antiaircraft guns of various calibers, backed up by gaggles of fighters. The Luftwaffe would be wait-ing in force for any Allied intruder.

The defenders would have plenty of warning of any Allied raid; the bombers had a long way to go out of their bases—mostly in Italy—and a long way to fly back. It was some four hours out to the target and another four hours back home, assuming the aircraft did not lose an engine and was not otherwise crippled. Much of the return trip would be in airplanes with dead and wounded crewmen, silent engines, and shot-up control surfaces.

Nevertheless, the USAAF decided to mount the attack on Ploesti; there was much risk, but it had to be taken. Too many Allied lives had already been lost. The British had already been fighting for the better part of four years, much of that time alone.

This would also be the first major European operation under-taken by the Army Air Force—as it then was—and the USAAF would never take on a tougher test. The Air Staff would plan the operation meticulously, hoping for success but intensely con-scious of the great risk.

The assault began with a series of relatively small attacks on the Ploesti complex, the early ones conventional high-altitude bombing runs. The first jumped off in May of 1942, a successful but relatively small-scale raid. Much more would be needed, and a series of other small strikes followed.

And then, in August 1943, came Operation Tidal Wave, a mass attack delivered at very low altitude—"naught feet," as the RAF would say. The raid was a maximum effort, 177 B-24 heavy bombers, their crews carefully briefed and rehearsed. Even so, the meticulous planning began to come unstuck early in the going. The aircraft carrying the hand-picked master navigator plunged abruptly into the sea on the way out, and the B-24 carrying his backup took enough time looking for survivors that it failed to catch up with the main force in time to lead the bombing. Other aircraft went astray in heavy cloud and finally found themselves bombing whatever they could.

Even so, the raiders did a great deal of damage to the Ploesti complex, but at terrible cost. The German defenses shot down fifty-four American bombers and badly shot up another fifty-three. The raids would continue nevertheless, but the question was plainly raised: What about the survivors of Tidal Wave and subsequent operations? Many of the tough bombers would survive crippling damage long enough to drop their loads on their assigned target but could not live long enough afterward to limp all the way home.

Sometimes wounded aircraft could hobble back to their home fields. Some others plainly could not. The crews of these bailed out into the unknown over Yugoslavia. If they thought they had a choice, they could try to nurse their crippled bird back across the Adriatic to a friendly field . . . and either make it back or not. Neither option was very attractive, but between the two, it was better far to jump into the unknown over land.

And so, with the heavy losses in aircraft suffered in the Romanian raids, Yugoslavia began to accumulate a substantial number of American aircrew. Some were captured by the Germans, of course, but over time hundreds sought and found shelter with the inhabitants. Almost always, they were made welcome, sheltered, and fed—even though the people in the small villages had little enough to eat themselves. The Americans were there to help them against the detested German invaders, and that was good enough for most of the hardy mountaineers.

There was some assistance from outside, especially from the Office of Strategic Services, better known as the OSS, America's foreign intelligence arm in World War II and a lineal ancestor of the CIA. OSS missions had dropped into Yugoslavia as they had into many other places, and here they had the heartfelt assistance of the Chetniks, the guerrillas who followed General Draza Mihailovich.

Here, a word is in order about the tangled world of politics in WWII Yugoslavia. Mihailovich's Chetniks were not only fighting the Germans but were also locked in a civil war with the Communists of Josip Broz, better known then and later simply as Tito. There was some belief that they were also collaborating with the Germans, but the truth of that—or at least, its extent—was much in dispute and would remain so, even after Mihailovich was "tried" and executed by Tito in a postwar show trial. That proceeding was probably no more than simply the judicial murder of one political rival by another. But even before it happened, the rivalry poisoned the political situation inside Yugoslavia.

For now, the pressing need was to get the surviving Americans out of the country. Understandably, they were getting more and more despondent, but more importantly they were experienced aircrew, extremely valuable assets to the fledgling USAAF. For Mihailovich they were also a ticket to a closer walk with the Allies, to more support for him and his men, who were short of everything from food to ammunition.

For both the Yugoslav guerrillas and the Allies, it was imperative to get the aircrew out. Easy enough to say; but a bigger question was, simply, how?

Gradually, many of the downed airmen had been gathered together in a place called Pranjane, more and more of them joined the group with each raid across the Carpathians, until at last the ever-growing total exceeded two hundred. Just feeding that many extra mouths was a terrible burden to the Yugoslav peasants, even though most of the Americans deliberately ate as little as they could get by with and helped out in the fields when they could.

The Germans knew there were substantial numbers of Americans somewhere about, although they did not know exactly where. At one point they even sent a message to Mihailovich; its sense was vintage Nazi, brutal and to the point: Hand over the Americans you're hiding, it said; if you don't, we'll mount a raid, destroy a convenient village, and kill a couple of hundred of its residents.

The senior American officer at Pranjane was appalled and offered to surrender his people to save civilian lives, but Mihailovich refused; it was not the American's decision to make, he said. And the next day the Germans did indeed invade a village and burned it to the ground . . . and killed everybody in it. The American officer cried.

The obstacles to a mass escape were many and obvious to everybody. Maybe you could lift a few men off by sea, but that was a very chancy business and first you had to get your people over the long, weary tracks to the coast. They could try walking out, but where? There were no friendly borders close by, so the chances of anybody staying out of a German POW compound were somewhere between slim and none. But there was a way.

Why, fly everybody out, of course. No chances to take on long hikes, just climb into a friendly American airplane and fly away home. Just like that. A C-47 could haul at least a couple of dozen airmen home, maybe a few more, depending on the length and quality of the airstrip. As it turned out, both were sharply limited.

Never mind that the Luftwaffe would probably interfere with any massive incursion by Allied aircraft; it would certainly try. Never mind also that substantial numbers of German troops were quartered in several villages nearby, ready to show up and rain on the American parade.

Worst of all, never mind that at present there was no airfield to land on, or any semblance of one, and no equipment save a few hand tools with which to build one. A proper job would require bulldozers and dump trucks and graders and such, heavy stuff that was not available locally and couldn't be air-landed. Now the C-47 was a wonderful airplane, a rugged workhorse that would carry about anything and take off and land about anyplace. But even this fine airplane took a minimum of about seven football fields to get itself into the air with any kind of a load.

There was also the matter of the Germans, who could be expected to appear at any hint of an escape or other Allied activity. And a village crammed with German troops, about 4,500 of them, was only some twelve miles away. There were other, smaller garrisons scattered over the area, including one no more than five miles distant. Only a short flight away was a Luftwaffe airstrip. There were enough German troops within a fairly short distance to overwhelm the local Chetniks, take the improvised strip under fire, and turn the escape into a disaster.

Even so, the work began.

The strip had to perch on the side of a mountain, there being little else in that part of Yugoslavia, roosting on a sort of small plateau no more than fifty yards wide and a little less than seven hundred yards long. Seven hundred yards was considered to be the minimum space needed by a C-47, so there was absolutely no room for error . . . or even for comfort.

The site was surrounded by mountains, forbidding at the best of times, and the plateau was flanked on one side by a sheer cliff and on the other by heavy forest. And, of course, nobody could predict whether there would be any wind at the time chosen for a landing, or if there was any wind, its velocity and direction. In short, the projected operation was fraught with an assortment of hazards; it would depend on an enormous amount of secretive and laborious air-strip building, the vagaries of nature, the alertness of the German forces, the weather, consummate execution by the C-47 pilots . . . and a great deal of luck.

The OSS mission looked for alternate sites, sending parties of airmen across the hills looking for something more inviting than the Pranjane area. The searchers returned to report that there were indeed better spots, but the nearest was fourteen hours' hard walk away. Switching to that spot meant not only leaving the relatively secure area around Pranjane but also transporting the wounded and injured among the aircrews along a murderous hike. Some could not possibly make it that far.

So it would be Pranjane.

Obviously, the quicker the work got started, the quicker it would be finished and the Americans could get out of Yugoslavia, but there were limitations on what could be done and when. One thing that was plentiful was strong, willing, eager labor. There were lots of American aircrew eager to get at it, some 250 of them, and they were joined by about 300 Chetnik soldiers and local villagers. The only "heavy equipment," however, was some sixty oxcarts brought in by the villagers.

The work went on from dawn until well after dark. The only interruptions came when an aircraft engine was heard; nearly everybody ran for the timber and hid until the plane went away. A few could stay in the open; after all, this was farming country and their presence would appear normal to a cruising Luftwaffe pilot. Swarms of people and a flotilla of oxcarts, on the other hand, would invite a visit from an army patrol, and there were too many German troops in the area for even the Chetniks to hold off for long.

All the work was done by hand; even the wounded did what little they could. With few tools available, the men dug up rocks by hand, and laboriously hauled and tamped down dirt to level the field. At the far end, they worked to cut down trees and root out the stumps, an enormous amount of sweat to buy a few more feet of room for the lumbering transports.

The C-47s were already planning to fly in with only a half-load of fuel, barely sufficient for the round trip; and the number of passengers was to be limited to about a half-load. Everybody knew what a crash during the operation would mean. A smashed-up, burning airplane almost certainly would mean a visit in force from the Wehrmacht.

Everybody waited with bated breath for a German patrol to stumble over their embryo airstrip or a German aircraft to spot the crowd of workers before they could run for cover, but the days went by and the strip miraculously neared completion without the Germans smelling a rat, until at last at date could be set.

It would be August 9. The C-47s would come in at night, their path lit by an improvised flare path. The wounded and injured would have priority, followed by those healthy men who'd been shot down the longest. Aircrew of the same plane would come out together with no preference made between officers and enlisted personnel, even though it took a lot longer to train a pilot than any other specialty.

With everybody's nerves on high alert, there was great excitement on the night before the evacuation was to start when the hammer of a machine gun broke the silence. What had happened? A German patrol? Was the chance for freedom gone at the last moment?

It wasn't, as a Chetnik officer soon explained. He is worth quoting: "Is no problem. No problem. One of my men saw something moving and challenged it. When it did not say anything, he fired his machine gun. Only cow. Now dead cow." Oh.

There was one more alarm, and it came on the big day itself, when two German Junkers transports and a Stuka dive-bomber flew directly over the strip. The ground was empty now, and seemed manicured and obvious to the Americans and Chetniks. That is, until a gaggle of loyal Yugoslav cows came to the rescue.

Deprived of the lush grass around the strip during the work, they were advancing now to satisfy their hunger, and did their part in making the field look properly agricultural and bovine. The German aircraft droned on.

Nobody was sure even then that no alarm had been given; some reassurance came when the Chetniks reported no unusual activity in the nearest German garrison. So the operation was on, and at the appointed hour four C-47s loomed out of the murk. There should have been six, but two had turned back with engine trouble.

The landing beacons were lit, oil-soaked hay bales and pots of oil given by the local villagers, and everybody waited anxiously. The first C-47 came in too hot. It hadn't left itself enough runway and aborted its landing, touching down and then roaring off again into the darkness to everybody's profound disappointment, but the next one made it. The pilots quickly learned to set their aircraft down at the very beginning of the strip, and all four were soon on the ground.

All four birds were quickly loaded, but before they left something happened that nobody who was there could ever forget. An American came to the door of one C-47, called to a new Yugoslavian friend, and threw the man his boots. And then there were Americans at all the aircraft doors, throwing boots and flight jackets, even socks and shirts to the villagers, many of whom had only a sort of felt slipper to see them through the bitter winter.

All four C-47s got safely airborne, after a difficult series of maneuvers just to get turned around on the edge of the narrow strip without tangling wingtips.

They had been lucky, and those on the airstrip wondered whether their luck would hold. It did. The evacuation flights continued the next morning, in daylight this time, six of them, covered by a swarm of very aggressive American P-38 and P-51 fighters. These aircraft occupied themselves by attacking any German vehicle or ground installation they could find for miles around, while the transport aircraft loaded up.

The C-47s would each take several more men than yesterday's half-load, leading off with the wounded who had missed evacuation the evening before. Yesterday's heart-warming farewell was repeated, as the airmen divested themselves of boots and all kinds of clothing useful to the Yugoslavian peasants who had been so protective of Americans in great danger, so helpful to those men so far from home.

Operation Halyard would continue. From an uncertain beginning to a triumphant end, the airlift flew out some 432 American aircrew, plus eighty other assorted Allied personnel—British, Canadian, French, and Russian. The Germans, in spite of their numbers, their equipment, and their nearby bases, failed to intervene.

Neither the rescuers nor the rescued lost a single life.

CHAPTER SEVENTEEN

Schloss Colditz and Other Delights

THIS BROODING CASTLE TURNED PRISON, A FORBIDDING *KONCEN-trationslager*, figures prominently in the tales of escape from Nazi-controlled Europe during World War II. First off, it was a real fortress, a strong, storied stone place of dungeons and towers and bars and great gates, an old frowning throwback to the pomp and violence of days long passed away.

It stands far out in eastern Germany, only some ninety kilometers from the border with what was then Czechoslovakia, and it became the centerpiece of the German prisoner-of-war system, the distant, desolate destination for the most dangerous Allied prisoners, that hard core who never stopped plotting escape.

It also held the *prominente*, those who were considered particular prizes of the Reich, men like Giles Romilly, Winston Churchill's nephew. A war correspondent as his uncle had once been—as Romilly had also been during the Spanish Civil War—he had been captured in 1940. It is well worth mentioning that he escaped after transfer to another camp toward the end of the war, getting clear to freedom by pretending to be a deaf-mute. Churchill blood.

This brooding, threatening stone pile was called Colditz Castle. The building of it had begun all the way back in 1014, and it was a storied place. Once it had been a hunting lodge and residence for the rulers of Saxony, known at various times as dukes, kings, and electors, this last title stemming from their role as one of the noble houses appointed to vote in the "election" of each Holy Roman emperor. Among the more famous rulers of this land was Augustus the Strong, well-known across Europe not only for his great physical strength but even more for his prodigious sexual appetite and potency, which produced a small army of offspring, all but one of them illegitimate. Legend has it that Augustus single-handedly increased the number of his subjects by at least 300, although that figure may have been enhanced just a bit by time.

By about 1800, the mighty castle was no longer a bright palace of government, merriment, and seduction; it had become a prison, a dismal, dreary place of bars and cells. It therefore seemed just the spot for the Third Reich to house those prisoners it most wanted to keep in secure confinement, and so it was dubbed a *Sonderlager*, a special camp. It was a long way for Allied aircraft to fly, a long way from help from the active Resistance movements in France, Belgium, or Holland, and its thick walls seemed virtually impossible to break through.

At the beginning, it was considered by the Germans to be virtually escape-proof, but it had its Achilles heel. Its hundreds of prisoners—about eight hundred at its fullest—were intelligent, inventive, and forever active, not the sort to be at all impressed by the castle's remote location and thick frowning walls. They constantly explored and discovered early on that much of the castle was uninhabited and had long been so, a rabbit warren of empty spaces: attics, cellars, and other unvisited places in which to produce and hide the essential tools of escape and evasion, to create all manner of false papers and phony uniforms and civilian clothing, places to work undisturbed by the jailors. Dutch sculptors even produced a pair of clay heads to cover prisoners' absence from daily headcount, the routine called *appell*.

The first successful escape came in the spring of 1941, when a French lieutenant disappeared from a column of prisoners on its way back to the prison from an exercise period in a field. He waited until a curve in the road briefly blocked the view of the accompanying guards, then jumped off the road and hid out in a house close by. In the end, he made it to neutral Switzerland. One source states that there were 316 attempts to escape from Colditz, with thirty-two of the escapers getting all the way home. One man, later head of the very successful MI9 escape apparatus, tried twice to leave Colditz behind him, both times dressed as a German guard. The second try succeeded. A French lieutenant appeared as a very respectably dressed woman and was well on his way to freedom until he/she dropped his watch. Some nearby British prisoners called out to her that she had done so, but she failed to stop, arousing the attention of the guards. Back to the castle.

RAF Flight Lieutenant Dominic Bruce, a very small man, crammed himself into a three-foot-square box with a file and a rope of bedsheets and had himself sent to storage. His escape was discovered the following day; his rope of sheets was hanging outside the window the next morning, and when the Germans looked at the empty storage box, they found it inscribed, *die luft in Colditz gefaellt mir nicht mehr. Auf wiedersehen.* "The air in Colditz doesn't please me any more. So long." He made it as far as Danzig, where he was arrested trying to stow away on a Swedish ship.

Some prisoners tried tunneling out or shinnying down ropes made of sheets or crawling out through the sewers. Some even tried getting out of Colditz as letters, hiding in mailsacks outbound for almost anyplace, since anyplace was better.

The prisoners, especially the British, got some back with homemade bombs, put together "like a milk carton," the targets being German guards in the castle courtyard below the cells. These homemade missiles were filled, of course, some with water and some "with excrement." It was only one manifestation of the British love of the gentle sport of "goon-baiting," what one officer called "a certain element of Brittery—a sort of ya-hooism against the only authority there was."

And then there was the master ploy, the "Colditz Cock," nothing less than a glider, to be built inside the walls and launched from the chapel roof, a spot out of sight of the Germans. It was the brainchild of two British pilots, one of whom was named Goldfinch, maybe an omen of success. Power for the launch would be provided by a counterweight dropping over the parapet of the roof, a metal bathtub full of concrete that would launch the glider into space at something approaching thirty miles per hour. Built to carry two men, the Cock was nineteen feet long with a wingspan of thirty-two feet. The notion was that the glider, launched from a sort of runway made of tables, would take two escapers away from the walls of Colditz and across the River Mulde, a couple of hundred feet below.

The materials to build the Cock were scrounged everywhere; prisoner-donated bedslats were excellent for making ribs, but the builders also used floor boards and anything else they could scrounge. Uninhabited parts of the castle yielded lots of electric wire to make control connections. The skin of the bird the builders made of blue-and-white-checked prison sleeping bags. The war ended before the Colditz Cock was ready to take wing. It never flew, but after the war a replica did, and quite successfully. Happily, Goldfinch and his partner were there to see it.

Simple laws of physics led to thoughtful plots of all kinds. For instance, everybody knew that sewage had to be gotten rid of, and that generally meant pipes leading to a sewer, a body of water, or a septic system. Wherever the pipes went, it was usually outside the prison, and where pipes went, determined, energetic men might also go. Escape attempts tried to follow the plumbing when it could, wherever the pipes might go.

There was no limit to the prisoners' ingenuity. French officers ran in money, information, and identification inside small welded boxes secreted in one-kilo tins of homemade "wild boar in sauce" sent by one officer's wife. The Germans never found out about this one, in part because the thoughtful wife would deliberately fail to sterilize the contents of the tin. By the time it reached Colditz, the tin's contents had turned; the German who explored it by punching it with a bayonet was rewarded by a vile stench, and promptly threw the tin away. The contents were obviously spoiled. The prisoners then fished the offending tin out of the garbage pile, opened it, and retrieved the little welded box.

The French were also the authors of an exceedingly complex tunnel attempt that led all over the castle, sometimes straight down, and also created a tremendous din of hammering and scraping. In time the tunnel—lit by electric light—extended out beyond the castle foundation, with only a few yards of soft earth left to cut through. Clothing and false papers were prepared for all two hundred or so French officers. It was slated to be an escape en masse.

It was obvious to the guards from the ceaseless din that some-body was doing an enormous amount of digging, but for weeks they could not find the source . . . until the day when, almost by accident, one section of the tunnel was revealed by the odd expedient of dropping a heavy clock-weight down a narrow shaft, knocking aside a barrier of boards and revealing a ladder that the guard cadre knew should never have been there. So near to frui-tion, the great French tunnel escape would never become reality.

Sometimes simple, boring routine provided a more useful opening for ingenious escape attempts. Witness what may be called "operation dirty laundry," the grand plan devised by Dutch Captain van den Heuvel. Van den Heuvel had observed that each week four Polish prisoners, shepherded by a couple of German soldiers, would collect the German officers' dirty laundry from a storeroom, the door to which opened outside the main castle fortifications. There the Poles would load the laundry into a pair of purpose-built wooden crates that took two men to carry them. They would then carry them a quarter of a mile from the castle, and there wash and iron the officers' uniforms under the more-or-less alert eyes of the NCO and a guard. What if, the prisoners asked themselves, we could transmogrify ourselves into a convincing group of four Poles and two Germans and just, well, walk out of this place? And so they set about it.

First they got into the storeroom where the dirty uniforms were collected. It was conveniently located directly below the office of the *Feldwebel* in charge of the laundry, which in its turn was just across the hall from the dispensary. The dispensary thus became the escapers' first target, and the first order of business was to get a man inside it. This was smoothly done by British Captain Kenneth Lockwood, who talked himself into a bed by convincingly faking severe stomach cramps. And, of course, during open hours he was visited there by a couple of sympathetic British friends, Pat Reid and Derek Gill. A sick man needs cheering up, doesn't he?

While nobody was looking, the visiting friends crawled under the sick man's bed and hid there. And then, in the dark of night after things were well locked up, Reid produced a set of purloined keys, opened the door to the *Feldwebel*'s office, and he and Gill entered, locked the door behind them, and went to work. They pulled the nails from the floorboards, lifted a few of the boards, and spent the rest of the night scraping away at the crumbling mortar underneath the boards. When morning appeared, they cleaned up, relaid the floorboards, replaced the nails, and hid any flaws by sprinkling on the floor a little dust (thoughtfully brought along for the purpose). They left and locked the office in time to show up for the morning *appell*.

The next night Gill and Reid repeated their act, until they had scraped a hole large enough to admit them to the store-room below, the place from which the collected laundry regularly departed. They left only a thin layer of plaster covering the storeroom ceiling and replaced the *Feldwebel*'s floor as they had the previous night. Meanwhile, elsewhere in the bowels of the prison, other prisoners were manufacturing uniforms, four Polish and two German, and the forgery department was cranking out flawless identification papers for the six men who were to make the break, three Dutch and three British.

Forgery attained the status of an art form among the Allied prisoners during World War II; even the multitude of seals so beloved of German bureaucrats could be fabricated by careful carving of a piece of linoleum into the proper stamp; appropriate inks were fabricated in all manner of ingenious ways, and paper and anything else essential could be stolen or traded for.

The escapers' final plan was to drop down into the storeroom from the *Feldwebel*'s office about two in the morning, then make the actual escape at seven that same morning, when the guard was changed. All went well at first. Everybody assembled in the office of the *Feldwebel*, and Lockwood locked the office door behind them; there was nothing to do now but wait. Reid and Gill were also along to furnish any help the operation might require. As it turned out, they were very badly needed indeed.

All was quiet until a prison alarm shattered the quiet of the night. It must have sounded like the Last Trumpet to the waiting men, and they could guess what had happened. One of the guard cadre had checked beds, and discovered that several of them were empty of people; now the search was on, but so far without any particular sense of urgency. Guards tramped down the hall outside the escape team's lair in the *Feldwebel*'s office but did not try to enter once they saw the room was locked. There was much searching of the prisoner spaces and common areas, but the Germans found nothing suspicious, and in time things quieted down.

That quiet could only be temporary, and the escapers and their confederates made the wise decision to carry on as planned. And so they pulled up the floorboards, cracked the thin skin of plaster below, and dropped through the hole into the storeroom. Behind them, Gill and Reid passed down the ersatz guard and Polish uniforms and the prefabricated laundry boxes, broken down in pieces for ease of movement, and carefully prefitted for quick and easy reassembly.

The escapers patched the ceiling behind them with plaster and water furnished by Gill and Reid, while Gill and Reid relaid the floorboards upstairs, locked the office door again and departed. And then, when the clock passed seven, the time had come to move. One of the Dutch officers—van Doorninck—dressed as a German *Gefreiter* (corporal) led the way, playing the role as German NCO-in-charge. Another Dutchman and three British officers manhandled the boxes, and Dutchman Donkers brought up the rear as a German private. The little procession marched out into the broad light of day and headed for the main gate.

They passed two sentries almost immediately, but neither one gave them a second glance. The guards were used to this routine little corporal's detail. It was a familiar thing, a dull, daily repetition; after all, why should a guard worry about four scruffy prisoners when they have an NCO and another guard watching them?

Then came the castle gate, where the escape team logically assumed the real test would come. "Corporal" van Doorninck, who spoke fair German, was prepared to give orders to the gate guard to pass them through but that proved unnecessary, for the sentry at the gate asked just the right question as they approached. "Are you going to the laundry?" Van Doorninck said they were indeed, and the sentry obligingly unlocked the gate and swung it open for them.

They were free.

They changed into civilian clothing brought with them and split up into three pairs, each composed of one Dutch officer and one British.

The pairs immediately went their separate ways, but the morning *appell* quickly revealed to the Germans that they were six prisoners short and a massive hunt was laid on immediately. One pair of escapers was caught that evening, the second the day after that.

But the third pair, van Doorninck and Bill Fowler, crossed the border into neutral Switzerland on the 15th of September, 1942, six days after they said *auf wiedersehen* to dreary Colditz Castle.

The stories of individual resourcefulness and courage are legion; tales of selfless willingness to help fellow prisoners, of bravery, endurance, and sacrifice far above and beyond the ordinary. The story of British Lieutenant Peter Allan is a good example of one who never lost heart or initiative over long years of imprisonment, of a long, dreary acquaintanceship with the fortress of Colditz that had begun on a gloomy autumn day all the way back in 1940.

By the time Allan tried breaking out of Colditz, there had been seventeen escape attempts in just six months. All were relatively amateurish and had failed; the time of sophisticated escaping had not yet arrived. But Allan had made it. He had gotten out of the prison complex by stuffing himself inside a sort of mattress thrown in the back of a truck. It was not his first try at escape; his first attempt, at a place called Laufen, was what had gotten him sent to Colditz in the first place.

And Allan spoke good German, a distinct advantage. Once clear of mattress and truck and on his way, profoundly weary, living on only a few potatoes stolen from a field, he took a chance on breaking three straight days of walking by flagging down a *kuebelwagen*, the German equivalent of a Jeep. Too late he realized that the two men in it were both members of the dreaded SS. He could only accept the ride, survive such limited conversation as there was, and on parting, "gave the best Hitler salute you've ever seen. I think I almost needed a new pair of shorts."

He made it all the way to Vienna, where he called at the American consulate, identified himself as an escaped British officer, and asked for help. He wanted only, as he told the consul, twenty marks to buy a meal and a ticket as far as the Hungarian border. The reply was a haughty, bureaucratic lecture about diplomatic status and an order to go away. He was caught soon after and returned to Colditz.

The ingenuity of the prisoners of Colditz—like that of other Allied POWs elsewhere, was as endless as their enthusiasm. They knew, as other prisoners did, that aside from giving the escapers a taste of freedom and a chance of getting entirely away and back in the war, and the satisfaction of outwitting the *Boche*, every escape contributed much to the war effort, and had to have saved Allied lives. Massive commitments of troops, money, and time followed any escape; those assets could have been spent by the Reich in much more useful ways. Especially in the latter days of the war, Germany needed more troops in a dozen different places, from Russia to North Africa. Some of those reinforcements would not come because they were hunting escaped Allied prisoners at home in their own Germany.

As one recaptured prisoner said, "It was worth it!"

It was.

Chapter Eighteen

If at First You Don't Succeed

Many Allied soldiers captured by the Germans never quit thinking about escape. Many tried repeatedly, one soldier at least eight times. He was never successful, but some tried again and again whether they made it or not. Douglas Bader (chapter 7) was one, as was Airey Neave (chapter 6). So was young Australian soldier Charles Granquist (chapter 5). These men were unusual, Neave for the scope of his attempts—trying to escape from the toughest German prison in a homemade disguise. Granquist stood out not only for his youth but also for his sheer persistence and savoir faire. Bader was a shining example for his sheer courage and persistence in the face of his handicap ... two aluminum legs.

Probably more typical of the average escaper or evader was an American grunt lieutenant named Walter Granecki, the kind of tough, dogged soldier who won the war against Nazi Germany.

Granecki and another lieutenant, Carl Pennington, went into the bag—as the British say—in May of 1944 at a point not far south of Rome. They had been out together doing a recon of a road ahead of an advance of American units, including tanks and trucks, and had found no evidence of either hostile troops or of mines laid along the road. The next step was to return to their outfit to report, but their trip was interrupted by the sudden appearance of German infantry. At first there seemed to be but one or two of the enemy, and Granecki and Pennington hunkered down and prepared to fight, but then the ground seemed to sprout more and more camouflage uniforms and burp guns until any resistance was obviously suicidal.

The two officers were herded back to a convenient wine cellar occupied by some hundred more German infantry. Any thought of escape vanished, at least for the moment, but that thought would return again and again. Afterward, they were moved from one prisoner *lager* to another and regularly interrogated. They gave the Germans nothing but name, rank, and serial number, and at last were shipped to a more permanent camp, this time a hole called Laterina, more than a hundred miles north of the Italian capital.

Laterina was not appealing. Breakfast was a cup of a vile something called coffee, but not readily identifiable as such. And that was all. The midday meal was bread and a cup of thin soup; dinner omitted the bread but featured somewhat thicker soup. Some of the prisoners must have welcomed their next move, although it was to an even more forbidding camp, a place called Mantova. Nobody had ever escaped from dismal Mantova, but this young officer was determined to try.

Illness delayed any concrete plans, illness in the form of a flare-up of a knife wound several years old. In great pain, Granecki was sent to the prison hospital, where he was cared for and better fed, even a bit of milk and some fruit and cake. While he was in the hospital, however, his comrade Pennington was shipped off to Germany with other prisoners.

As he got better, thoughts of escape occupied Granecki, and when he could move he began to roam the hospital corridors, trying to memorize his surroundings, looking for the weak spot, the flaw in security that would help him break out. When a nurse saw him one night and asked what he was doing, he complained that he couldn't sleep. He threw away the sleeping pills he was given and kept on prowling.

He found his weak spot in the hospital cellar, where everybody was sent when the Allies bombed the nearby railroad terminal. One window had no bars on it, maybe the start of his escape route. He conferred with other prisoners, American and British, who had escaped and been recaptured. But before they went back behind bars or wire, they had traveled and learned much about the Italian countryside and its people, some of whom, he learned, wanted nothing whatever to do with Germany and, in fact, favored the Allies. There were even armed Italian partisan bands out there, men who believed the only good German was a dead one, and killed them whenever they could. One of the things he learned would serve him in good stead later: the poorer the Italians were, the more likely to favor the Allies over their Fascist government and any German at all.

So Granecki made his preparations, acquiring items of civilian clothing—among other things, he traded a pen for a pair of shoes—and learned what he could of Italian by swapping English lessons for instruction in Italian from hospital workers. He could not wait too long to make his break, for he could not know if and when he might be shipped to Germany, as other prisoners had been, as his buddy Pennington had.

And so at last, on the night of August 14, he made his try. Wearing his civilian clothing under his uniform, he carefully worked his way through the hospital corridors, passed a German sentry asleep on a gurney, got to the basement, and climbed out his unbarred window. Once outside, he still had to negotiate two fences; the first, seven feet of barbed wire, he managed by crawling along the fence to a gate, then crossing the fence by climbing over a stone pillar supporting the gate.

He wasn't out yet. The real obstacle lay beyond, another tall wire fence also topped with barbed wire. This one he started to climb using its grillwork, but he hadn't climbed far before his foot banged on the gate and kicked open a small door. He gave up climbing and walked through to freedom. He made the best time he could through the rest of the night, not sure where he was going, but eager to put as many miles as possible between him and the hospital guards.

With the morning, he found himself close to a farm; a little village lay beyond. He was ravenously hungry, and decided to try the hospitality of the farmhouse. An old man came out shouting, and Granecki tried to cool things by pointing to himself and saying "American." At this the man smiled and relaxed. "Escaped?" he said, and Granecki said that was so. Smiling, the man motioned at Granecki to wait. Granecki could almost taste the bread and maybe other good things when an elderly women came running from the same farmhouse, pointing in the direction the old man had taken, and shouting "*Tedeschi! Tedeschi!* Go!" Granecki knew what that meant, "Germans! Germans!" and he went.

He quickly stashed his uniform under some bushes and, as American GIs were wont to say "unassed the area," trying to hurry without looking like it. He got clear, but that didn't solve the problem of something to eat and maybe a place to sleep under cover.

Remembering what he had learned from other escapers, he finally chose the poorest farm he could find. He could see no men, only a young woman with a child, and an older women engaged in feeding chickens. He walked up to the women and said, "Eat, American." The older woman responded, "Parachutist?" And Granecki answered, "Prisoner, American."

The response was magic. He was showered with bread, toma-toes, and figs, and he repeatedly expressed his gratitude, "Good, thank you." The two women, obviously dirt poor, even tried to give him money, which he refused. That same scene was repeated over and over again at small farms over the next few days; one farmer even gave Granecki another shirt.

Granecki asked repeatedly about partisan bands, but nobody knew, or would say, anything about them, until at last a farmer agreed to lead Granecki to a partisan band. It took two days of hiking before they came upon the band of a partisan leader called, of all things, Franco. Franco promised Granecki lots of action and Granecki "enlisted" in the band. Until, that is, the band staged a raid on a power plant and provoked a major German response. The word was passed to Franco that some two hundred troops with artillery were on the way to hunt him down. Since his band numbered fewer than two dozen, the option of standing his ground was a quick road to suicide. He gave the order to scatter.

So Granecki was on the road again, traveling fast, maybe faster than he should have. He began to travel through towns, instead of skirting them, taking chances by moving in daylight as well as darkness, and at last his luck ran out. Italian soldiers had so far shown no interest in him, but it was an Italian army patrol that finally stopped him, a patrol, ironically, that was looking for German deserters. Since he had no identification, he was arrested and turned over to the Germans and, worse luck, he was on his way back to Mantova. That was bad, but it would get worse.

He would not be long there, for only a few days after he returned to the camp, all the prisoners were marched to the railroad station and loaded into boxcars. Their destination was even worse luck, a prison camp deep in Germany. In his cramped boxcar, Granecki's thoughts turned again to escape and he care-fully surveyed the car in which he and thirty-five other men were penned up. They were in two groups, one sealed off with barbed wire at each end of the boxcar. In between the groups were the partly open boxcar doors and five guards.

Each end of the car had three small windows, each closed with a sort of wooden shutter and snap catch. Granecki open two of the little shutters, to find both windows closed with iron bars. He did not try the third window. But that night, with all three shutters kept closed against the chill, it began to get stuffy in the car, and somebody asked that a window be opened. A British officer obligingly did so, and then quietly said, "There are no bars on that window."

Ah! From what Granecki could see, there were no outside guards, and the window was wide enough for him to wriggle through. "I'm going out," he told his fellow prisoners, and two British officers said they wanted to go too. And so the three—Granecki, Trevor, and "Shorty," as Granecki called him—crawled out into the cold darkness, clung to the side of the car, and wondered where they were. In the gloom, they could see a road and a river and distant mountains, but nobody knew how far they'd already traveled, so they could be still in Italy or maybe Austria . . . or maybe, God forbid, already over the German border.

At last, as the train seemed to slow a little, all three men jumped out into an inhospitable world of darkness, rain, sleet, and patches of snow. All through the day and the next night they kept on, until they found a friendly Italian family. Welcomed and well fed, they spent the night asleep on heaps of straw and pressed on. The second night they tried a group of houses and found welcoming families, including a British soldier who had escaped over a year earlier. The soldier said he could find a guide who would guide the fugitives to the Swiss border. Shorty and Trevor welcomed the idea, but Granecki did not.

He was worried about his wife, who could not know whether he was even alive, and he was determined to get back to American lines. And so he headed south again, relying on the good will and hospitality of Italian farmers. They did not fail him, and one gave him a letter to a partisan leader.

This band was more substantial than Franco's, some forty men and eight women, everybody dressed in a strange mixture of Italian, German, and British uniform. When Granecki told the band's leader that he wanted to get back to the American lines, the leader matter of factly agreed. He had a group leaving the next morning, including several American aircrew who had parachuted to safety when their aircraft crashed in the mountains. The way was bitter cold, steep and rough, and still the group had to avoid falling into the Germans' hands and getting shot by the Americans. Granecki was grateful for the headscarf given him by one of the partisan women.

And at last the group found an American outpost, including two machine guns that covered their road to freedom. Granecki shouted down the road, "I'm an American," he roared, "I'm an American officer," and the outpost heard him. They carefully waved the tattered refugees in, and Granecki was taken to the command post of the sergeant in charge, some short distance behind the outpost. Like good sergeants everywhere, this one put important things first and was engaged in feeding Granecki when the sergeant's boss, a lieutenant-colonel, appeared.

Old habits die hard, and Granecki snapped to attention and saluted. Eyeing this ragged apparition in a headscarf, stuffing his face on army rations, the colonel burst out laughing. "What are you?" said he, and hearing who Granecki and the others were, and what they had been through, the colonel immediately telephoned for medical help and more food.

Granecki started to cry.

A short time later, Granecki was able to make the call home he had so long dreamed about. At first his wife thought the call was somebody's vile idea of a joke, but Granecki was able to persuade her that he was indeed real, back from the dead, and would be home soon . . . by Christmas.

CHAPTER NINETEEN

The Magicians

ONE OF MI9's MOST IMPORTANT FUNCTIONS WAS HEADED BY A genius named Christopher Clayton Hutton, known to all and sundry as "Clutty." He was something of a stormy petrel, in trouble at various times with various police departments, all three services, MI5 and MI6, Scotland Yard, Customs, and various government departments. He was also, however, far too valuable an asset to MI9 to let such minor peccadillos interfere with his work.

> *His boss described both his value and his temperament exactly in a letter written—significantly—to an army provost marshal officer: "This officer is eccentric. He cannot be expected to comply with ordinary service discipline, but he is far too valuable for his services to be lost to this department."*

He was indeed valuable, of immense importance to the entire war effort, and he was also very much the "eccentric." Hutton was a single-minded man, who operated out of a bunker he had built in a field near Wilton Park, ostensibly for privacy. There, on the edge of a derelict graveyard, he developed all manner of useful items.

He started logically with WWI escape tales, books he got the British Museum to scrounge for him out of the multitude of secondhand bookstores in the Bloomsbury district of London. He then got this accumulated lore summarized by students at Rugby, and flew off to Bartholomew's, a famous mapping firm in Edinburgh. The firm showered him with maps, and he went to see a friend in the textile business who got him some silk. Clutty had already decided that silk was the very thing out of which to make maps for aircrew: it was hard to damage; unlike paper, it didn't rustle when it was concealed somewhere in a flyer's uniform; and it held a clear, useful impression, once he had added pectin to ordinary printing ink. Silk was more expensive than ordinary paper, to be sure, but silk was more durable, easier to hide, and safer to use.

He found use for paper as well, especially when a friend at his club told him about some special Japanese pulp that made thin, nonrustling paper. This paper could be used for maps, too, especially tiny ones hidden between the front and the back of innocent-looking playing cards, which were also produced and made their way to Nazi prison camps.

Clutty made himself master of the miniature compass business as well, enlisting the highly competent help of a veteran London firm called Blunt's. After Clutty found a way to provide a thousand feet of steel strip, Blunt's promptly turned the raw material into five thousand little steel ribbons, suitably magnetized. The next step was producing various types of tiny compasses, some carefully secreted inside buttons or collar studs (then widely worn); at need, you could scrape off the paint covering the face and navigate.

Hundreds of thousands of Clutty compasses masqueraded as buttons of various sizes. To use the compass, you had to turn the front of the button to remove it and reveal the compass face. Just in case the Germans thought of testing big buttons, Clutty thoughtfully had the button covers manufactured with left-hand threads. A nosy guard's curious twisting of the button's face simply tightened the button's face even tighter.

Some compasses were simply tiny brass cylinders with a minute, luminous needle, small enough to fit within the bowl of a pipe or even inside a fountain pen; at need, you could stash them almost anywhere. At least once, three British soldiers in a small boat navigated their way to England from Dunkirk with one of the little cylinders.

More than two million compasses of various types were produced for MI9 during the war, including over 1,300,000 of the handy little brass cylinders. A handy substitute was the ordinary razor blade, hung on the end of a thread or a string so that it would swing. Clutty was able to arrange for all ordinary razor blades sold in armed forces stores to be magnetized; north was always the end of the blade on which the maker's name began. Then there was the steel pencil clip that also doubled as a compass, balanced on the point of its own pencil on a tiny indentation in the clip.

Any one of these made a fine companion piece to a tiny hacksaw, only 4½" × ½", punched with a hole at one end so you could hang it down your trouser leg or suspend it out of sight in about any narrow crevice. The skinny saw could be fitted with a homemade handle or used without. In the carnage of the Arnhem battle, a least once the little tool did yeoman service as a surgical saw. And later, Clutty got some Gigli saws, surgical wire saws with a textile cover, suitable for concealment as a bootlace.

Clothing was a more difficult proposition. He tried his hand without much luck at replacement British uniforms that might be altered to at least resemble a German uniform. A more promising project was a "present-from-home" blanket. Sent to a prisoner by a fictitious relative from a fictitious home, the blanket bore a pattern that you could follow in cutting out a civilian-type coat . . . when you were ready to sew, you got the pattern to appear by soaking the blanket in cold water.

But Clutty's pièce-de-résistance was the escape box, modeled on the common box of fifty cigarettes but a little larger and made of plastic. In it, the well-equipped escaper had hard candy, chocolate, halazone and benzedrine tables, fishing line and hook, soap, razor with magnetized blade, matches, rubber water bottle (capacity about a pint), and needle and thread. Produced by the hundreds of thousands, and used by American, British, and Commonwealth troops, it gave a man all he needed to sustain himself for forty-eight hours or so while he hid out to let the post-breakout excitement cool a little. A welcome addition was some money and a map of whatever country you were flying over.

Some footwear was built with cloth leggings that could be turned into a reasonably convincing semblance of a civilian shoe. There were hollow heels in which you could hide contraband, and replacement uniforms sent to prison camps often were designed for easy conversion to civilian clothing. He also fabricated a special escaper's knife, an all-purpose tool that neatly included everything from saws and a lock pick to a wire cutter. If you could get it into a POW compound, it was a tremendous asset.

Hutton had specialized help. Among other assistance, he used the ingenuity of a professional magician called Jasper Maskelyne, who developed all manner of ingenious hiding places: hollow cricket bats, real money stashed in Monopoly games, maps hidden in playing cards, and the like. There are all kinds of fantastic stories about Maskelyne, tales of wonderous feats of hiding whole masses of vehicles, people, and other things, tales that in some cases look very much to have been vastly inflated. Nevertheless, some of his contributions to the shadow war remain real and valuable.

Hutton's achievements were demonstrably the real thing. There were even phonograph records designed to split into halves to hold false documents; closure of the split hid the documents entirely.

Afterword

THESE ARE ONLY A FEW OF THE STORIES OF GALLANTRY, DARING, and sacrifice that have come out of the escapes and attempts to escape during World War II. All of the people who populate these pages share enormous courage: the military and civilians alike; the rescuers and the rescued; those who made it back and those who didn't; those who came home to well-deserved applause, and those who died miserably alone, unknown, in the cellars of the Gestapo or the Kempetai.

All of them leave a great legacy, a precious heritage that those of us who come after must learn, value, and remember . . . and try our very best to be worthy of the words a great United States Marine said of his men:

UNCOMMON VALOR WAS A COMMON VIRTUE.

BIBLIOGRAPHY

Alexander, Larry. *Shadows in the Jungle*. New American Library, 2009.

Berry, William A. *Prisoner of the Rising Sun*. Macedon, 1993.

Bradford, Andrew. *Escape from Saint Valery-en-Caux*. History Press, 2009.

Brickhill, Paul. *Reach for the Sky*. Naval Institute Press, 2001.

Byers, Ann. *Rescuing the Danish Jews: A Heroic Story from the Holocaust*. Enslow, 2011.

Chancellor, Henry. *Colditz*. William Morrow, 2001.

Clark, Albert P. *33 Months as a POW*. Fulcrum, 2004.

Dear, I. C. B. (ed.). *Oxford Companion to World War II*. Oxford University Press, 1995.

Dorril, Stephen. *MI6*. Free Press, 2000.

Fishman, Jack. *And the Walls Came Tumbling Down*. Macmillian, 1983.

Foot, M. R. D., and J. M. Langley. *MI9 Escape and Evasion*. Book Club Associates, n.d.

Freeman, Gregory. *The Forgotten 500*. New American Library 2007.

Galland, Adolf. *The First and the Last*. Ballantine, 1954.

Granquist, Charles. *A Long Way Home*. Big Sky, 2010.

Heiman, Judith M. *The Airmen and the Headhunters*. Harcourt, 2007.

Johnson, Tony. *Escape to Freedom*. Leo Cooper, 2002.

Kerr, E. Bartlett. *Surrender and Survival*. William Morrow, 1985.

King-Clark, Rex. *Free for a Blast*. Fleur de Lys, 1988.

———. *Jack Churchill, Unlimited Boldness*. Fleur de Lys, 1997.

Lineberry, Cate. *The Secret Rescue*. Back Bay Books/Little Brown, 2014.

Lucas, Laddie. *Flying Colours*. Wordsworth, 2011.
Lukacs, John D. *Escape from Davao*. New American Library, 2007.
Michno, Gregory F. *Death on the Hellships*. Naval Institute Press, 2001.
Neave, Airey. *They Have Their Exits*. Leo Cooper, 1953.
———. *Saturday at MI9*. Pen and Sword, 1969.
Pape, Richard. *Boldness Be My Friend*. Headline Publishing Group, 2007.
Philpot, Oliver, *Stolen Journey*. Dutton, 1952.
Rawicz, Slavomir. *The Long Walk: A True Story of a Trek to Freedom*. Lyons Press, 1997.
Redford, Duncan. *A History of the Royal Navy, World War II*. Tamus, 2014.
Reid, P. R. *Colditz, the Full Story*. Pan Books, 2002.
Simpson, Paul. *Prison Breaks*. Robinson, 2013.
Sullivan, George. *Great Escapes of World War II*. Scholastic, 1988.
Williams, Eric. *The Wooden Horse*. Collins, 1979.
Young, Peter. *Commando*. Ballantine, 1969.

INDEX

Arranzaso, Alberto, 37–38
attention deflected, 109–10
Augustus the Strong, 208
Australia, 42
Australia (HMAS), 158

B
B-17 Flying Fortress, 152
Babcock, John, 154
Bader, Douglas, 219; bi-plane
    crash of, 85; captivity of,
    86; collaborator betraying,
    87; court-martial testimony
    of, 88–89; escape planning
    of, 86–87; espionage charge
    against, 91–92; going home, 92;
    goon-baiting of, 89–90; legs
    amputated of, 85; replacement
    legs for, 87; ruckus caused by,
    88; Stalag Luft III move of, 90;
    Stalag VIIIB move of, 90–91;
    tunnel plans of, 89–90
baggage, 13
bagpipes, 181, 189–90
Baker, Sergeant, 35–36
Baker, William D., 152
baloot (delicacy), 136
banzai Nippon (long live Japan), 39
barracks, 4, 21
barter system, 10
Barton, B. J., 189
Bataan Death March, 155
Baxter, Tom, 138
Bay of Salerno, 187
Becquet, Antoinette, 108
BEF. *See* British Expeditionary
    Forces

Besley, Laura, 147–50
Best, Werner, 46
Big X, 2
bi-plane crash, 85
Birk, Larry, 108–9
Black Watch regiment, 117–18, 126
Black Widow fighter, 99, 101
blitzkrieg, 118
blood chit, 79
Boelens, Leo, 128, 130, 139
Bogart, Humphrey, 158
bombing mission, 104
bombs, homemade, 210
boot soles, 10
Borneo, 40–41
Bowfin, USS, 139
boxcar transport, 223–24
Brac (Yugoslav island), 189
Bradford, B. C.: capture of, 121;
    escape of, 119–20; European
    travel hazards of, 120;
    German patrol stopping,
    120; important posts of, 126;
    imprisonment of, 119, 122;
    midget sailboat voyage of,
    125–26; military family of,
    118; prison parole of, 123;
    rope of sheets of, 122; ship for
    Algiers, 123–24; Spanish not
    spoken by, 121–22
Bradley, Alan, 175
brass cylinders, 229
Brazil Maru, 129
brickwork foundations, 4
Britain, 83; airmen, 114; demolition,
    186; Empire, 126; escapers
    back in, 30–31; fabricators, 26;